Rise Above:
Conquering Adversities

Greg Little

Printed in the United States of America on acid-free paper.
First published by Dog Ear Publishing
4010 W. 86th Street, Ste H
Indianapolis, IN 46268
www.dogearpublishing.net

Edited by Kathy McClure, Risa Bruner and Isidor Muniz
Copyedited by Dorothy Davis

ISBN: 978-145750-486-0

Distributed by:
Falling Star Publishers
P.O. Box 923
Columbus, MS 39701

Author's Website:
http://drgregdlittle.com

CONTENTS

To order additional copies of
Rise Above
by
Greg Little,
call 1-662-275-3940

drgregdlittle.com

ACKNOWLEDGEMENTS

THERE ARE SOME people who without their guidance, assistance and encouragement this writing would have been impossible. First and foremost is **Jesus Christ**. Without Him any attempts to overcome or even face any of the adversities mentioned in this book would have been pointless.

My son, **Patrick**, had to grow up so very fast. He had to do this, many times on his own, at a very young age. He has become a very talented musician, who has been an excellent example of how to gather many friends . . . be one. Several months after he was born, he gave to me the greatest title I have ever known, *Daddy*.

Much of this writing was turned into a readable work due to the tillage of my editors, **Kathy McClure, Risa Bruner** and **Isidor Muniz**. Their insight and ability to make this a more scholarly writing cannot be overstated. Any attempt to adequately thank them for their many comments and suggestions would be futile.

The first letter in this writing would never have met the ink if not for my friend, **Dale Henry**. It was his idea that I develop a program on overcoming adversity, as well as a book of the same. When I first met Dale during our doctoral study in 1989, we began a friendship that many should emulate. As you read in these pages, he will always be on the front row in the theater of my life.

I would be amiss if I omitted one very important person, **you**. This book is in your hands, because you may have overcome an adversity. Perhaps you are facing one. It is my hope and prayer that the writing in these short chapters will give you the *how to* or *how to leave alone*. Either way, please remember, as you will read later, that you are only limited by your ability to adapt.

INTRODUCTION

OCCASIONALLY MY PHONE will ring or I will receive a *Call for Papers* from an association or company requesting that I speak at their conference or convention. It will often be for a couple of 90-minute breakout sessions, sometimes a keynote address or sometimes for all day, 6-hours. The one at the other end and I will discuss my fee. She then states that she will arrange my flight, hotel, and all necessary details.

That all sounds great. I, as do most speakers, get a rush from being in front of an audience. That was not always the case. To be honest, there was a time in my life when *I knew* I would never have done such a ridiculous stunt as speaking in public . . . to any public.

All of us face some sort of adversity in our lives. The severity of that adversity can only be determined by the one faced with the challenge at hand. Some are born with physical and mental challenges, which others would consider life-altering. However, the one born with the challenge may not even consider it an adversity. It has been my pleasure to know such people.

Most of us, at least once in our lifetime, are faced with self-doubt. That's ok. Only then do we find the need to dig deep into our inner being and find something, which is often a nugget we never knew existed, that gives us the realization that our challenges can be met.

Though not always conquered, this at least gives the courage to face the self-doubt. It is rare that we look into our inner being and find more self-doubt.

This book is about how to look into our inner being. Specifically, how I learned to look into my inner being. For a very long time I did come across that rare find. . . *additional* self-doubt. That self-doubt was the result of a severe speech impediment.

When I say *severe*, I am not taking the word *severe* lightly. In all likelihood, you control your speech. You control what you say, the volume and the rate you say it. For those of us with speech impediments, mine was stuttering, our speech often controls us.

It is important to emphasize that mine *was* stuttering. No, I'm not cured. That is not an option. With the help of a very competent speech therapist, I learned that mine can be con-trolled . . . and by me. From the time I learned to talk until I was about 18 years old, my speech was a constant thought. Other people who stutter have conveyed the same dilemma to me. Nothing could be worse . . . I thought. In the summer of 1972 something happened to me that was worse. For me it was a motor vehicle accident that resulted in my receiving three skull fractures, a bruised brain, and an 8-day coma, as well as having to relearn to walk and talk.

What could be worse than that? On November 24, 1991, I found that something. My 18-month old son died. What could be worse? I know people who have had multiple children to die. One lady I know had 5 children to die. I know a man whose 18-year old son went to a party many years ago and was never heard from again. No one saw him at the party; conse-quently, no closure. It can always be worse.

Another's adversity may seem worse than yours, but you know your own adversity. You may have known it so long that if you have not overcome it, at least it is in your *comfort zone*. This book is about how to overcome self-doubt, or at least put it into your comfort zone.

PREFACE

JUNE 17, 1972. That night my life was changed forever. That as you may know is the date of the Watergate Break-in . . . which has nothing to do with me.

However, late that night I was involved in a motor vehicle accident (MVA), which resulted in my receiving three skull fractures, a bruised brain and having to relearn how to walk and talk.

After being thrown into the backseat of my 1968 Pontiac Lemans, I lay unconscious for six hours before being found. Unconscious and bleeding from my left ear, but — luckily — no one else was involved. You probably have surmised by now that I was not wearing my seatbelt. Why should I? At 18 and a three-week graduate from high school — I was invincible. Nothing was going to happen to me. I was even attending summer school at Northeast MS Community College (NEMCC) in Booneville, which is 20 miles from my hometown of Corinth.

Earlier that day, I had gone to Pickwick Lake in Tennessee with my friend Dan to meet a couple of female friends, who were staying with one of the girl's parents. I told my parents that if I didn't get back that night I was going to stay overnight in our cabin. That evening my friends and I threw a Frisbee near the Pickwick Dam. The lights were bright at the dam, so we could see the Frisbee very well and didn't realize how late it was.

After the girls left, Dan and I started our thirty-mile journey home to Corinth. We decided to make a couple of stops at some nightspots along the way. Since Dan was an excellent drummer both times the bands asked him to sit-in with them for a few songs.

Oh, excuse me. Seems I'm getting ahead of myself. We need to go back a few years.

THE LACK OF CONFIDENCE

TO FEEL CONFIDENT, it is always good to begin anything with a positive initiation, such as school. September 1960, my academic career began in the first grade. I suppose that would be a good place for school to start.

Sitting at the breakfast table with the normal anxiety a first grader might have on his first day of school, I found it difficult to eat my breakfast. Thinking his little boy was in need of a good breakfast before his first day of school; my father verbally scolded me until I ate my breakfast.

After breakfast, my mother took me to school. At this particular school, the first thing all school kids did was stand in line to have our picture made. We then went with our mothers and were shown the way to our rooms. After everyone was as comfortable as possible, the mothers would leave.

Everyone was adapting to the new environment, except for one boy, who cried when his mother started to leave. The mother was told that he would be all right after she left. So she left. He was not happy. He kept trying to go to the door and continued to cry. Not knowing what to do, the first grade teacher sent for the principal. We could all sense this was going to be trouble.

The principal, an elderly woman, came to the room. The boy kept crying. She took out a wooden paddle — from where I don't know. She sat in a chair facing the class, bent the boy over her lap and told everyone to watch. She applied corporal punishment to the five or six year old young man's bottom.

He then did what one would expect. He was crying more by now! Perhaps he learned a good lesson . . . what that is I'm sure I don't want to know.

As for me, I was sitting in the back of the room watching this take place and had handled the situation rather calmly, until the principal left. I then proceeded to throw-up . . . on three girls. Naturally, my father was contacted and told that I needed to go home due to being sick. So much for my first day of school . . . and that darn breakfast.

Stuttering is an awful burden for a person to carry throughout life. There was never a time in my childhood, when I cannot remember stuttering. Others in my family have had this same affliction; some as far away as a fourth cousin.

This would echo the findings mentioned by Drayna in Phend (2010) that stuttering may arise from genetic defects in a basic metabolic process in which cells dispose of waste. Though these findings are significant, it should be pointed out that the genetic defects in this study appear to play a role in 5% to 10% of the individuals in the study, who stutter.

This study will allow our greater society to no longer stigmatize stuttering as simply a disorder where one 'needs to slow down' or that one 'needs to relax,' according to Dr. Drayna.

Children can be cruel. Sometimes the cruelty is not intentional. Please note that I said *sometimes.*

During elementary school, junior high or high school, my **fear** of giving a book report or reading in class was more than most people could comprehend. Certainly, most students dreaded these times, but **true fear** was not a part of their experience.

There were actually times in junior high school, when I was scheduled to give a book report on a certain day that I would tell my mother I was sick, just so I could avoid going to school. What I was doing was lying to avoid facing my fear, which only fanned the flame of anxiety for future speaking episodes.

There were times when I would come home from junior high school and actually cry due to my believed helpless affliction of stuttering. Kids would laugh at me or mock me. I would be called upon to read in class, which was always a humiliating experience. My knees would shake, and my voice would shake. Obviously, there was a whole lot of shakin' going on. I digress.

When the class would have to read aloud one paragraph per student in order up and down the row, I would count to myself how many paragraphs or students it would be before it became my turn. I would read the paragraph over and over in my mind. Usually, I would mentally read the paragraph very fast in order to put this terrible task behind me.

Little did I know this was the worst way to overcome my challenge. Not only was it the worst, it was not going to work . . . ever. However, it was the only option I thought that might work.

It was not until years later that I learned that our weaknesses are our strengths taken to the extreme. Hang with me on that one. You will read about that later. There would be times that I would sit in class praying the class would end before it was my turn to read.

Sometimes, a teacher would call on students at random. During my junior year in high school my English teacher, Mrs. Sharp, would do just that. She knew I stuttered; yet, she called on me to read aloud just as much as the other students. She would even ask me to breakdown the parts of the sentence I had just read. One might say that Mrs. Sharp showed no mercy.

Later in life I would learn during speech therapy that what Mrs. Sharp did was the exact thing she should have done for me. Specifically, when people who stutter avoid a speaking situation, all they have done is increase the anxiety for the next time they speak.

Virtually all people who stutter and discuss this with me have the same experiences. They would actually worry in the morning, while going to school, if they would be called upon to speak some time during the day. Non-stuttering friends, who can in no way relate, have said to me, *Just talk.*

They reinforced to me what would be difficult for me to comprehend . . . it is actually THAT easy for them. As is a fear for most people who stutter, answering the telephone can be a dreadful act in itself.

There were times in my childhood that I would stammer with my speech, which is normal for young children. When doing this in front of my father, he would reprimand me with a grimace on his face that would be impossible to forget. Consequently, if I stuttered in front of other people, I would subconsciously see the grimaced face on my listener. That only compounded my apprehension at my next occasion to speak. It was as if stuttering entered my life passively through the backdoor.

Let's stop for a minute. Before you think, *poor, poor, pitiful Greg*, or think that your parent(s) did the same type of behavior, it's important to realize that, when you were born, you did not come with instructions. In all probability no one gave your parents a handbook and told them how to be a good parent. The only parenting examples they had were the ones their parents gave them. As my good friend, Dr. Isidor Muniz reminded me, *the apple doesn't fall too far from the tree.*

Answering the telephone by merely saying, *Hello* was many times a tremendous fear. During my youth, and even up to my senior year in college, having to answer a telephone with a word beginning with the letter *h* was a dreadful experience.

There was an incident in my youth when attempting to answer the telephone in our home by saying *hello* that I hit a block. A block is a term used in speech therapy to describe an attempt to pronounce a word but the one speaking hits a verbal wall or block. My block was the *H*. Someone made a telephone call to my home, and all that would come from my mouth was, *H......h...h....* So, in an attempt to help, my father, who was in the other room, yelled, *Hello?!*

Well, believe it or not, the fact he could say, *Hello*, did not help me at all in my attempt to get through my block or say the word; even though I was thrilled that my father could say it.

There was a period during my senior year in college that I was again having a devil of a time saying *Hello* to begin a telephone conversation. So, in lieu of *Hello*, I was using the word, *Yeah*.

Now there is an easy word to say; however, it is not very refined. What if after applying for employment I received a phone call from the prospective employer and answered the telephone by saying, *Yeah!* The words on the other end of the line would probably be, *Oooooh, I have the wrong number.*

Trust me – asking a girl for a date in high school was an enormous undertaking. I would sometimes mentally practice the phone call for hours. Little did I know this actually enhanced my anxiety. My greatest fear was that the girl's mother – or worse, her father would answer the phone, and I would have to ask a parent if I could speak with my potential date. Oh, death where be thy sting?!

2

TO GAIN ACCEPTANCE

AS CHILDREN OR adolescents, we all want to be accepted by our peers. All of us want friends. Very few people desire to go through life alone. Most people gain friends by communicating – talking. Talking is an act, which most people take for granted. We learn it as an infant. Most people just do it . . . many times without effort.

When this act of talking is a challenge, fear raises its ugly head. Years of visiting several speech therapists provided me with numerous words of wisdom regarding stuttering. One of the most eye-opening statements came from Dr. Bob Rhodes a former professor of speech therapy at the university level. Dr. Rhodes once told me that *stuttering is something someone who stutters does, when he tries not to stutter.*

It may take some time for that to sink in, but it's the truth. A person, who stutters, should focus on the tools of speaking clearly rather than focus on the pending dysfluency. Once during a speech therapy session I went into a long one-way discussion as to *my theories* as to the origin of my stuttering. The therapist stopped me in mid-flight and told me that the origin of my stuttering was not important. The solution was important. That made a significant impact on me.

Most problems in life regardless the issue, are prolonged by people focusing time and energy on the cause rather than the solution. We want to point a finger and blame someone when something goes wrong in life. It is much more convenient to blame a person, when we really do know the cause of something. Too often people are afraid to speak-up with what could be a solution. They are afraid of what people might say about them. Don't let that stop you. We are going to talk about you anyway.

Baseball. I've always been fascinated with that sport. That was my aspiration . . . to be a professional baseball player. Shoot! Only one thing kept me from realizing that dream. Specifically, I wasn't very good.

I did play Babe Ruth League Baseball, age 13-15. Oh, I wasn't too bad my last year. I mainly played outfield and occasionally first base, when the regular first baseman, Greg Tull, pitched. My claim to fame in the Bath Ruth League was my last year. I led the league – in singles. Consequently, the thought that I would never be a professional baseball player became reality.

So, here I was growing-up as a skinny kid . . . and I mean skinny. I was often too ashamed in the summers to go without a shirt. When I graduated high school, this humble fellow stood six feet tall and weighed 125 lbs. Only years later would it be known to me that no one, with the exception of me, cared about my appearance. They were too busy focusing on their appearance or simply did not care. Now add the fear of speaking — anywhere.

So, how was I going to fit-in, be accepted by my peers. I've got it! I'll become the class clown. It started in elementary school, and when it stops, I'll be sure to let you know. There were so many of my teachers, who wanted to pull their hair out – or even worse, pull MY hair out! I gave them fits, but I was constantly doing funny things to cause my classmates to laugh.

It's important to know that it was not my conscious purpose to use my humor to gain acceptance. Perhaps somewhere in the back of my mind someone said this would work. Kids did seemed to accept me, and it was my way at least I thought, of getting friends.

My 6th grade class performed an operetta, Tom Sawyer. I was given the part of *Jim*, the African-American assigned to perform chores for Tom's mother. As you can guess, I really *hammed it up* for that performance. My 6th grade teacher, Ms. Waldron, when recording my grades on my report card, always gave very poor grades to me for conduct, sometimes even marking it in red! I say, *gave* poor grades to me for conduct. Actually, I *earned* every one of them.

During my 5th and 6th grade years, my mother took me to visit a chiropractor for my stuttering. She had heard that a chiropractor could help to cure stuttering. She believed my sessions with the chiropractor helped my speech. I didn't think so, but my back felt great!

During my 9th grade year, my parents were advised to take me to a psychiatrist for my stuttering. This was in the late 60's. Someone, perhaps a physician thought perhaps my stuttering was a mental problem. Meeting with the psychiatrist on two occasions was pointless. My respect for psychiatry is to the utmost, but believing it will cure stuttering, at least in my case was nil.

Well, here comes junior high school. Oh, no. Going to a new school and meeting kids from another elementary school in Corinth. How was this kid with low self-esteem going to fit it? My subconscious was thinking. I'll make them laugh. I did, and it worked.

You may be wondering why it's so difficult in school for a child, who stutters. Having spoken to other people with speech impediments over the years, we have virtually the same issues.

Imagine being in class and not understanding all of a lecture from a teacher. No problem, right? Just raise your hand and ask the teacher a question. Everyone else does. If you have a speech impediment, raising your hand and asking a question is virtually not an option. So, you often take a test without totally understanding at least one aspect of the subject.

By the time high school arrived, the grooves of my life had been set. I was a comedian. Everyone has heard the term, *comic relief*, used by people needing to experience laughter in order to purge their stress. Well, providing comedy relief purged my stress.

Getting through high school can be fun. It also provides its share of challenges. All teenagers want to fit-in. Their bodies are changing. Hormones have gone into overdrive, and acne pays a visit. Dating will soon be on the horizon. Boys talk a good game about that.

I mentioned earlier *comic relief* as my strong suit, at least the strongest suit I had. You may ask, *How could someone with a speech impediment have been a class clown?*

Glad you asked. Most of my humor was visual. Sure, there were times when I told a joke or some verbal prank. Most of the times it was easier for me to *do* something funny.

My sophomore year in high school was when I developed a rather good impersonation of a fly. That's right. You read that right. *A fly*. That impersonation would get laugher from a statue. So, I went through high school with the nickname, *Fly*. Not very sexy, huh?

3

NOTHING COULD PUT ME BACK TOGETHER

GRADUATING FROM HIGH school on May 26, 1972, my intentions were to enroll in college and pursue a major in recreation . . . or law enforcement. Don't ask, *Why law enforcement?*

I'm sure I couldn't tell you. Perhaps it was to be the opposite of what I had been for years . . . law abiding. Perhaps somewhere my mind was thinking that a criminal could be made to laugh so hard until he surrenders . . . before he wets his pants!

No matter what my pursuit, I knew I had to complete my core college, i.e. English, Western Civilization and Speech first. I was hoping that those courses might be lesser evils if taken in the summer at a community college. There was one only 20 miles from my home. So, a week after high school I was enrolled to take English Composition and Western Civilization. My grades weren't bad. I had B averages in both classes. Then it happened . . . .

On Saturday, June 17, some friends and I planned to meet at the Pickwick Dam in Tennessee. We threw the Frisbee, got a bite to eat . . . the normal things teenagers do. I told my parents, *Not to worry. If it got too late, I would stay over with some friends.*

Not *staying over*, was a big mistake. After spending time at the dam, the girls left to go back to their cabin. It had gotten late. Dan and I went to a couple of night spots. Dan was an excellent drummer and the bands asked him to sit-in for a few songs. It was getting really late.

I rode with Dan in his car back to his home where my car was waiting for me. Getting into my vehicle for the drive to my parents' house, I realized I was sleepy, but my home was only about five (5) miles away. The drive should be no problem. Picture this . . . an 18 year old kid driving around 1:00 AM, sleepy and the air filled with a very heavy fog. Anyone with half-a-brain would be wearing a seat belt, right? Well, back in 1972 seat belts were not mandatory as they are now, and no one ever accused me of having half-a-brain. Oh, I suppose that last part has changed.

Driving very fast, I came to a shortcut to my parents' house. It would be the longest *shortcut* of my life. About two miles from home my late model Pontiac Lemans went off the right-side of the road. My two-door vehicle had bucket seats — the type of bucket seats that leaned forward to allow someone to get into the back seat. The seats were not made to fold backward.

Going off the road on the right-side, my vehicle hit an embankment. This threw me forward with my face, specifically my left eye, hitting the rearview mirror. The impact was severe enough to throw my body back onto my seat and bend the seat so that it was lying flat in the backseat. My bucket seat was designed to fold forward not backward; yet, my body impact changed that. The vehicle was not finished.

After hitting the embankment it went across the road, only now without a driver. The vehicle's fast movement threw my unconscious body into the back seat. The vehicle then ran over three fence posts as my body was thrashed around in the backseat cracking my skull in three places, tearing a muscle in my back and bruising my entire brain, and as mentioned earlier, my left-eye was now bruised shut.

My auto accident happened in a pasture belonging to a neighboring farmer, who later stated he heard a noise that night but thought it was his cows. I somehow take offense to that. Just kidding.

Six-hours later, in his pasture that farmer found my car with me in the backseat. He hurriedly telephoned a funeral home. In 1972 ambulance services in my hometown were provided by funeral homes. He hurriedly told the dispatcher, *There's been a wreck on Salem Road!*

He then hung-up the telephone . . . without telling the dispatcher *where* there was a wreck on Salem Road. So, here comes the ambulance driver not knowing which route to take. Naturally, he took the route closest to the funeral home . . . which was the longest route to the accident. I cannot blame them. How were they to know?

The driver of the ambulance was John Paul Anderson, who three weeks earlier was my marching partner at our high school graduation ceremony. His co-worker in the ambulance was Ronnie Jones, who in 1968-69 was on the same baseball team with me in the Babe Ruth League. Naturally, when they left in the ambulance, they had no idea it was me in the accident.

When they arrived, the Sheriff's patrolmen were waiting for them. John Paul and Ronnie took my broken body out of the totaled vehicle. They carried me from my vehicle, with a backseat smeared with dried blood from my left ear as a result of skull fractures, and they strapped me onto the gurney and rolled me into the ambulance.

John Paul quickly drove the ambulance to the lone hospital in my hometown. In 1972 this hospital had no neuro-surgeon, which my appearance and X-rays indicated was very much warranted.

The medical staff put all appropriate steps hurriedly into motion. The Baptist Hospital in Memphis, TN was alerted that a transfer was in the making. Now, someone had to inform my parents. It was Sunday morning around 7:00. Mom and Dad had just gotten out of bed to prepare for coffee, the Sunday newspaper, breakfast and church. Peggy Harris, who was a nurse on duty at the hospital and a friend to my family, knew my condition was serious.

She first phoned her cousin, Buddy Bain, who with his wife, Kaye, lived three houses from my parents, and asked them to drive my parents to the hospital in Corinth, then to Memphis. Hopefully, they could see me briefly prior to the transfer to Memphis. Peggy knew that after hearing the news my father would be in no condition for the 96-mile drive from their house to Memphis.

Buddy and Kaye Bain prepared for the drive to Memphis while hoping and praying for a miracle. Peggy now had the job of informing my parents of something that would change their lives. Dad answered the phone. Peggy said, *Howard, this is Peggy. Greg has been in an accident. He's here at the hospital, and it's serious.*

Dad put his hand on the wall to brace himself. Peggy continued, *His skull was fractured and we're transferring him to Baptist Hospital in Memphis. Buddy and Kaye are coming to your house to bring you and Earline to the hospital. You need to get here as quickly as you can, because we really need to leave soon.*

It was now my Dad's job to relay the message to his already tearful wife. My parents packed what they could with their minds racing with questions and stress like they had never experienced. Buddy and Kaye quickly arrived to escort them to the local hospital. My total time at my hometown hospital was at the most an hour.

After triage care was given to me, John Paul Anderson, who had driven the ambulance from the accident site to the hospital and assisted in triage, waited to drive the ambulance to Memphis. His patience wore thin. While giving my parents as much time as possible, John Paul knew that he was working against time. He told the emergency room personnel to tell my parents that he could wait no longer.

Peggy climbed into the back of the ambulance with me. From the Magnolia Hospital in Corinth to the Baptist Hospital in Memphis is 93 miles. John Paul drove it in 47 minutes. Yes, he did. He later told me that his foot never left the floor of the ambulance. Peggy would later tell me that every couple of minutes on the journey John Paul would ask, *How's he doing?!*

13

Arriving at the emergency room entrance of Baptist Hospital, medical personnel opened the door to the ambulance. Opening the door and seeing the obvious injuries to my skull and head, an ER doctor turned to John Paul and asked, *Are you the one from Corinth?*

John Paul acknowledged. The physician replied, *You got him here just in time.*

That was June 18. My parents arrived with Buddy and Kaye a little later that morning. My parents were allowed to see me briefly as I lay on the gurney. Neurosurgery was needed – quickly. There was just one problem. Several other patients with head trauma were also in need of neurosurgery – also quickly. Patients, mostly teenagers, were being admitted to the head trauma ward at an alarming rate. This was primarily due to motorcycle or automobile accidents. Wearing motorcycle helmets and seatbelts had not been made into law in 1972. They were just considered *good things to do.*

The next day, June 19, a prominent neurosurgeon, Dr. Matthew W. Wood, Sr. performed surgery on my brain to relieve pressure, which had developed from the contusions. He was assisted by Dr. Semmes from the Semmes-Murphy Clinic, which was across from the Baptist Hospital. Following the surgery Dr. Semmes sat down with my mother and asked, *Are you the mother?*

She nodded, *Yes.*

He then told her that I had a severe brain injury, but they are doing all they can. Dr. Wood later told my father that the surgical team thought I would die in surgery.

Now came the hard part. The wait. While I lay in a coma in the intensive care unit (ICU), my family along with the many friends who came to visit, could do nothing but wait, cry . . . and pray. From what I was told, a great deal was done of all three. I was in a coma for eight days. Every two hours visitors were allowed to see me for five minutes each.

Trapped Youth Remains 'Poor'

By Jerry Robbins
Staff Writer

Eighteen - year old Greg Little, who lay unconscious in his wrecked car for some six hours before being found, remains in critical condition in a Memphis hospital.

He apparently lost control of his car on the Oakland School Road while returning from a Pickwick outing.

The late model Pontiac left the road, crashed through a fence and overturned down an embankment.

Pipeline construction workers found the car, discovered the youth inside unconscious and called a Coleman Ambulance around 6 a.m. Sunday. He was rushed to Magnolia but immediately transferred to Baptist Memorial Hospital in Memphis.

A member of the family said Greg had told his parents when he left Saturday afternoon for an outing at Pickwick with friends, "not to worry" if he didn't return home around midnight Saturday. He might stay overnight.

He was apparently returning home around 11:30 p.m. when the accident occurred, but was not found until Sunday morning.

Baptist Memorial Hospital in Memphis told The Daily Corinthian this morning that Greg's condition is listed as poor. He

Corinth was admitted to the local hospital after receiving multiple bruises and lacerations in an automobile accident at 3:35 p.m. Friday.

Three people were injured in an automobile accident Saturday at 3 p.m.

Francis Wren, Route 2, Rienzi was treated at Magnolia Hospital.

pital at 3:10 p.m. for head injuries and referred to Baptist Hospital in Memphis.

G.A. Wren, 73, Route 2, Rienzi, was admitted to Magnolia Hospital with multiple injuries to the head, arm and knee and lacerations of the forehead.

Marvin Lovelace, age 40, Route 1, Corinth was treated

for lacerations of the forehead and discharged following the same accident.

A motorcycle accident at 5:30 Saturday resulted in injuries to a Corinth youth. Tony Lee Harris, age 13, was treated for lacerations of the thigh and fingers and transferred to Baptist Memorial Hospital in Memphis.

Teen Hurt

Greg Little, 18-year-old Corinth High School graduate was injured in this late model Pontiac on Oakland School Road late Saturday night. He is listed in "poor condition" at Baptist Memorial Hospital in Memphis.
(Daily Corinthian Photo)

Greg Remains Unconscious

Greg Little, 18-year old Corinth youth injured in an automobile accident here Saturday night, remains in a coma in the intensive care unit of Baptist Memorial Hospital in Memphis.

Howard Little, Greg's father, told the Corinthian today that "there is no change in his condition this morning".

My head was severely swollen from the bruising, and my left-eye was also swollen from being bruised from the initial impact. Family members told me that my mother cried for eight days straight. My parents and brothers later told me that I did move my right arm during my time in a coma.

Also during that time, my cousin Jackie came to visit. By now he was a sheriff's patrolman in Memphis; consequently, it

Today's World

Injured Teen In A Coma

Greg Little, 18, who was injured in an automobile accident here late Saturday night remains in poor condition today at Baptist Memorial Hospital in Memphis.

Doctors performed surgery on Greg yesterday and termed it successful but reported no change in his condition. He remains in a coma.

Greg is the son of Mr. and Mrs. Howard Little of Frankland Drive in Corinth.

Mr. Little said this morning the family was "feeling the prayers" of people who are concerned about their son.

He said he is still convinced "the Lord is still on His thrown and in command."

was easier for him to visit than many of my family from Corinth. Jackie and I have always been fans of the St. Louis Cardinals baseball team. During one visit with me while I was still comatose, Jackie held my hand and said, *Greg, the Cardinals are really doing well.*

I squeezed his hand. That would be the foundation of what I would teach in workshops years later – people in a coma are often able to comprehend much more than we might give them credit.

Each day after seeing me, Dr. Wood came into the waiting room to speak with my parents. He would hold his hands apart a few inches and say, *Greg has improved this much.*

His hands moved slightly further apart each day.

Greg Seems Better, Family Has Hope

Greg Little, hospitalized since last Sunday at Baptist.
Memorial Hospital in Memphis following an auto-
mobile accident, remains in a coma today.

Howard Little, Greg's father, told the Corinthian
today that his son's condition is "slightly improved
and he is making a little progress."

Mr. Little expressed his appreciation to the many
people here that have been concerned about Greg's
condition and asked that "prayers be continued"
because they were being answered.

During the eight-day coma, my oldest brother, Ray, stayed in a chair outside the door to my room. Sitting, waiting and like everyone else, praying.

My other brother, Tom, wrote a letter to Archie Manning, who was going into his second year as quarterback of the New Orleans Saints. Tom described my condition to then 23 year-old Manning and requested an autographed picture. A few weeks later a large envelope came to the hospital room from the New Orleans Saints Football Team. Inside it was a picture of the young quarterback.

It was autographed, *To Greg, Archie Manning.*

I've collected several hundred autographs over the years, but none as important as that one.

On June 27 a family member came into my room to have her five-minute visit. My right-eye was open; I was awake. She ran down the hall screaming, *He's awake! He's awake!*

All of my immediate family came to ICU. Though my left-eye was still bruised shut, my right-eye was partially open. Using his thumb and index finger, my father opened my eye fully. I was able to look around the room. It would be nice if I could remember what I saw, but I have no idea.

I stayed in intensive care a few more days and was then transferred to a private room. The swelling on my eye was beginning to subside, but I was now paralyzed on the left side of

17

ARCHIE MANNING   QB   NEW ORLEANS SAINTS

my body from my face down to my legs, and my ability to speak was completely gone. I was unable to make a sound.

Oh, I was also bald from having my head shaved, except for the hair at the very base of my skull, for the surgery. I know that's not very important, but for an 18 year-old kid . . . .

The paralysis and inability to speak lasted for three weeks. Because I was now in a private room, it was easier for people to visit, but because I was unable to speak, no one knew how much

I was able to remember. Poor short-term memory following traumatic brain injury (TBI) is virtually a given. During my hospitalization, my memory would be worse than terrible at times and not too bad at others.

One day a couple of friends from high school, Danny Patterson and Rich Heyer, came to see me. Each shook my hand and told me his name. Shaking hands, as long as it was with the right hand, was the one thing I could do now. I wanted to say, *I know who you are! Tell me what's going on back in Corinth.*

Unfortunately, communicating was not an option. During the first few weeks, not being able to walk was one of the worst things on my plate; however, for me not being able to speak was even worse. We control our environment by our ability to communicate. Not being able to control my environment was frustrating. I remember vividly lying in bed, not being able to speak and thinking about my speech impediment. I remember saying to myself, *I sure do miss it.*

A bit of a contrast from what you read earlier, huh? It may seem rather odd to imagine me lying on my hospital bed and actually missing my speech impediment. You have probably heard the phrase; *I complained that I had no shoes until I met a man, who had no legs.*

Everyone we meet has strengths, and everyone we meet has needs. Everyone has emotional or physical baggage. We just need to learn how to concentrate on changing those needs or baggage into challenges . . . and those challenges into opportunities . . . and those opportunities into strengths. Easier said than done? Oh, much. Just stay with me . . . .

Other problems surfaced. While I was in ICU or shortly afterwards, my physician prescribed penicillin to combat infection. What no one knew was I am allergic to penicillin. My physician was a Boy Scout leader, and his troop went on a camping trip. When he returned, the penicillin had caused a rash in my stomach and mouth, as well as a fever. The fever got so high that my arms and legs had to be packed in ice.

The medications along with the head injury at times would make me delusional. My parents informed me that when an attendant was in my room changing the linens, I said to him, *I was shot by the same man that shot President Kennedy.*

Also, and I remember this, when I was taken for a stroll in my wheelchair out of my room one time, I saw Dr. Wood in at the nurses' station and said, *There's the man, who cut my hair!*

I mean really, was a little haircut much of a price to pay for my life? Now it was time to rehab. Due to the torn muscle in my back, my left arm was essentially worthless. Pictures taken of me after my hospitalization revealed a stark contrast in the size of my arms. My right-arm, though very thin, was much larger than my left-arm. During my hospitalization in Memphis, a physical therapist came to my room a few times to provide range-of-motion to my left-arm. That arm would be the last *visible* damaged part to heal.

Re-learning to walk would be a huge undertaking. Two physical therapists came to my room twice a day. With one on each side and each holding onto one of my arms, they essentially dragged me down the hallway. From one end of the hallway to the other we slowly moved as I made any effort I could to step. Very gradually, my ability to walk returned.

Another physical therapist would come into my room and work on my torn back muscle. He provided range of motion to my left arm, which was half the size of my right arm due to the torn muscle on the left side of my upper back. This torn muscle made use of my left arm impossible. Ranging my left arm, which had no muscle tone, was painful. That physical therapist could have been employed by the CIA to interrogate prisons. However, his efforts were not in vain. Half of this reading was typed with my left hand. Before this physical therapist came into my life, my left-hand could not pick-up a straw.

There was a cute petite dark blonde nurse, who looked to be in her mid-20's, working on my floor while I was in Memphis. I know I was 18 years-old with a shaved head and three long scars on my scalp lying in a hospital bed, but I was still an 18 year-old male with hormones. It was nice to see this lovely fair maiden, whenever she came into my room. She always smiled and was full of life. To borrow the words of Zig Ziglar, *She smiled so wide; she could have eaten a banana – sideways.*

My little broken brain would think absurd things like, *Oh wait 'til I get out of the hospital!*

Though highly unlikely, but surely not impossible, maybe one day she and I could go on a date. One day, while in my private room, I said something to my Mother about how pretty the nurse was. Mother agreed and then nonchalantly informed me the nurse I was referring had conducted a procedure for me, when I was in a coma that involved a bedpan. *Oh death where be thy sting?!* Following this enlightenment my previous aspirations for this nurse diminished.

The outpour of concern from my family and friends was a huge boost for my recovery. Cards, letters, flowers and visitors came seemingly non-stop. At one point there were two full large grocery bags of cards and letters that I had yet to read. Without our knowing, hospital aides took the grocery bags out as trash. After learning what had happened, my mother threw a fit. She went down the hall and gave the aides *a piece of her mind.* I'm being kind.

In the late 1940's and early 1950's my father was involved in state politics. Consequently, he had made friends with people who continued to be in the political realm. Senator James O. Eastland, who at the time was the United States Senate Pro-tem, telephoned my father twice from Washington while I was comatose to inquire about my condition.

Buddy Bain, who with his wife had taken my parents to Memphis on June 18, was a radio personality in Corinth. He conducted a daily radio program during which he would play records but primarily talk about events in North Mississippi. Buddy would call the waiting room in ICU and ask one of my brothers or my Dad, *How is he doing? You must tell me something. People are calling the station non-stop.*

My hometown newspaper, The Daily Corinthian, ran an article about my recovery or the lack thereof almost every day.

That summer was my first year to coach Little League Baseball. My team was the Crackers, and the players were ages 7-9. A few articles were published about my team and their injured coach. One day the newspaper displayed a picture of my team praying for me after a victory.

Remember Our Coach

Members of the Crackers baseball team in the Southern League pause for prayer. The prayer was for their coach, Greg Little, who remains hospitalized from an auto accident. The Crack won the game in the final inning. was for the league lead.
(Daily Corinthian Photo

One day when I was alone in my hospital room, it rained. The hard rain was hitting the windowsill. I knew that day that I was going to recover. I cannot explain that. Just knew it.

One night in Memphis I woke and said, *Cecil Bennett. I've got to see Cecil Bennett!*

From what I was told, I then lay back down and went back to sleep. He was a man from Corinth, who sold insurance to my father. I saw Mr. Bennett about one time a year, at the most.

Team Wins, Stops To Pray For Its Coach In Hospital

Greg Little's team hasn't lost a game this season.

But he doesn't know it.

Greg lies unconscious in a Memphis hospital. He is the victim of an automobile crash.

The 18-year-old had coached the Crackers to a perfect season.

Yesterday's game was the biggest of the year. It was against the Chicks. Both teams were undefeated.

When it was over, Greg's team was the victor. The win came in the final inning 5-4.

Greg doesn't know his team has the league lead. But the team knows about Greg.

After yesterday's win, the tea ed to the side, knelt and prayed Jaudon. Their prayers were fo He is their coach and their And they miss him.

In the moments of triumph, t never forgot Greg. He has been panion, pal and tutor.

The baseball contest Thursd challenging. But for Greg, his ch is for life.

Greg's father, Howard Little as plainly as it can be spoke feel the prayers of people."

Yesterday the team added its for Greg.

The next day, my father made the 96 mile drive back to Corinth to check the mail and go by our house. While at the post office, he happened to be there at the same time Mr. Bennett was also checking his mail. Dad relayed to Mr. Bennett that I woke the night before and called out his name. Mr. Bennett said, *I asked my church to pray for Greg last night.*

Two months passed, and I had improved enough for Dr. Wood to transfer me back to the local hospital in Corinth. I rode with my parents from the Baptist Hospital on the 93-mile drive to the Magnolia Hospital. What was so odd, due to the past two months having been spent without listening to the radio, virtually every song played on the radio was new. We had ridden for about an hour before I recognized any song, specifically Gilbert O'Sullivan's *Alone Again, Naturally.*

The Magnolia Hospital, specifically room 411, would be my residence for the next ten days. I was going to my hometown and would be able see my friends. My family physician, Dr. Frank Davis, met with me shortly after admission. Dr. Frank, as everyone in our rather small town referred to him, ordered a soft diet for me. This is in stark contrast to the food

23

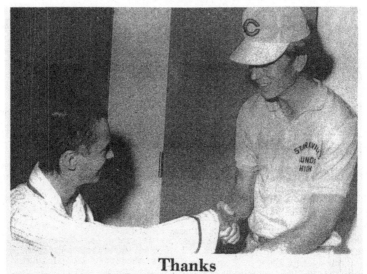

Thanks

Greg Little, a patient at Magnolia Hospital, shakes coached prior to an automobile accident. The Crack-hands with Joe Jaudon following the presentation by ers won the Southern League regular season title Jaudon of a team baseball. Autographed by members with an undefeated 9-0 record.

in Memphis. There I was given regular food, which the rash inside my mouth and stomach made food almost impossible to swallow. The soft diet was a much welcome change.

To address the rash in my mouth and stomach Dr. Frank had me drink four 8-oz glasses of buttermilk every day. Let's stop right here. To some people, buttermilk is delicious. That's alright. They have the right to be wrong. I must admit the buttermilk did help in ridding me of the internal rash. Hopefully, by now the medical world has developed a more tasteful means to address internal rashes. However, at the time I felt battery acid in lieu of buttermilk would have been more appealing.

In 1972 the Magnolia Hospital did not yet have a physical therapist; so, Dr. Frank advised my family to obtain a baseball-size rubber ball for me. My Aunt Pauline believed the initial rubber ball given to me was too hard; consequently, she found one that was not too hard, too soft or too large. Aunts have a way of doing those things. I was to use the rubber ball to re-build the strength in my left-arm.

Dr. Frank told me to slowly squeeze the ball and pull my arm backward; then, bring my arm forwards and slowly release the ball. I was to do this as much as I could when watching television or listening to the radio. It worked. Strength in my left-arm slowly returned; even though to this day I cannot sleep on my left side.

How would loss of weight be addressed? I was unable to eat solid foods. Dr. Frank wrote a prescription for Vivonex, which is a vitamin supplement — and a good one. The only problem at that time was that its taste wasn't pleasing to my palate . . . not as bad as buttermilk though.

The hospital pharmacist, Steve Knight, was a friend of mine. He was eight years my senior, but we had developed a friendship through mutual friends. Besides, Corinth is a small town. Steve, upon seeing Dr. Frank's written order for the Vivonex, filled the order . . . but he mixed it with a milkshake. That allowed the Vivonex to go down much easier.

One day I was lying in my bed watching television by myself. Steve came into my room and sat in a chair across the room. He said, *Man, I just wanted to get away and take a break. It's (work) been non-stop today.*

Granted, Steve and I had developed a friendship, mostly through sports, but he was coming to my room for a break. I was a patient in the hospital; consequently, I was *work*. This experience compelled me to emphasize in my workshops – to give someone worth, give them your time. That's what life is made of — time.

One of the best ways to gain respect of someone is to pay attention to them. By paying attention to someone, you give them worth. If you want to win someone over, show them that you find worth in them. One of the best ways to do this is pay attention to them. To go even further the best way to pay attention to someone is to listen to them. Listening should not be confused with hearing. We hear sounds with our ears, but we listen with our entire body. More will be mentioned of this later.

Earlier, you read about the picture Archie Manning sent to me, when I was in intensive care. That picture would mean even more, when I was able to learn more about Archie Manning from a good friend of mine, Art Bressler. Art played football at Ole Miss. He played guard and was All-SEC for three years. Following his college years, he played two years for the Calgary Stampeders in the Canadian Football League.

He was a freshman during Archie's senior year. Archie was also assigned to be Art's big brother on the football team. Unlike other varsity players, who might take advantage of underclassmen, Archie told Art that all Archie wanted him to do was get his mail and laundry.

Archie made it a point to convey to people they have worth. During Archie's senior year at Ole Miss, he was being touted for the Heisman Trophy. If his left arm had not been broken in Ole Miss' homecoming game against the University of Houston, Archie's chances for the Heisman might have become a reality. One day, following a home game in Oxford, the reporters were hovering around Archie asking questions and taking pictures. Art and his Dad were across the room watching the attention the All-American quarterback was receiving. As he was answering a question, he looked over a reporter's shoulder and saw Art with his Dad. Archie yelled, *Mr. Bressler!*

He then left the reporters and walked over to where Art and his dad were standing and shook Mr. Bressler's hand. Art would later tell me that act by Archie made a very significant impression on his dad. By paying attention to Mr. Bressler, Archie conveyed to Mr. Bressler that he had worth.

Since his playing days at Ole Miss, Archie married his college sweetheart, Olivia, and the couple has three grown sons, Cooper, Peyton and Eli. The later two play professional football. No matter how old the sons are, Archie and Olivia never end a telephone conversation without saying, *I love you.*

Wouldn't it be nice if all parents and children, regardless the age, did that. We do love our kids, right? When are they too old to hear it?

One day there was a knock on the door, and a pretty young lady, Cindy Spear, came into the room. She and I dated the previous fall. She came with another young lady to visit me. It was really good to see her. Then unexpectedly the door opened. There stood a nurse, who smiled and asked in what seemed a voice loud enough to be heard in the next county, *Have you had a bowel movement today?*

Don't get me wrong. I know I'm not the first person to have natural bodily functions, but there IS a reason doors are put on bathrooms. It seems sensitivity training for medical personnel was not always emphasized in 1972.

As stated earlier, my auto accident occurred on the night of June 17, 1972, which is also the date of the Watergate Break-in. Due to being in a coma for the first two weeks and ICU for two additional days, fourteen days had passed before seeing anything on the television. One more time . . . *at least fourteen days had passed* . . ., because when I finally was transferred to a private room in Memphis, I was still paralyzed and unable to speak. That made requesting a program or asking someone to even turn-on the television rather impossible.

When I was finally able to watch television, the news media coverage was in full force covering the break-in, ultimately leading to the resignation of President Nixon. By the time I was transferred to Magnolia Hospital, updates of Watergate were consuming the news. There was one problem. I had no idea what in the world Watergate was suppose to be. One day my older brother, Ray, was in my hospital room with me. I said, *Ray, all I hear on the news is 'Watergate.' What is Watergate?*

Ray, who at the time lived outside of New Orleans, LA, said, *You don't know what Watergate is?*

I replied, *No.*

Ray continued, *Well Greg, there's a huge gate in New Orleans holding in the water from Lake Pontchartrain, and they're debating whether they should open the gate. If they do, it will flood the city, but it will fertilize the marsh.*

Remember, I had recently received a traumatic brain damage, which meant the apparatus used to process information was not working properly. Consequently, for a narrow second in time opening a gate at Lake Pontchartrain seemed possible.

During the last four days of my 10-day stay at the Magnolia Hospital, Dr. Frank allowed me to go home for 1-2 hours per day. That was a much welcome offering. Getting to eat my Mom's cooking and being able to lie in my own bed would be a small piece of Heaven.

Each day, Dr. Frank would come to Room 411, check how my left arm was responding, look at my chart to review my vital signs, ask a few questions and tell me he would see me the next day. One day my brother took the few clothes I had home for my Mom to wash them. The next day, Dr. Frank came in, did his usual ritual but this time ended with, *Greg, put your clothes on.* I was going home!

I replied, *If I had any, I would.*

Pajamas and a robe would suffice. After 40-days I went home. Before being discharged, my vital signs were taken one last time. The two that I remember was: height 6'0" and weight 110lbs. That was more than thin.

Due to the torn muscle in my back, my left-arm was still virtually worthless. My mother had to assist me at mealtime with anything involving a knife. One-hand just couldn't cut it. She also had to button my shirts and, due to me losing so much weight, had to put a safety pin on my pants in order for them to stay up. Cards, flowers, friends and family were still regular visitors. That went a long way in lifting my spirits and allowed me to realize how much the act of caring can play in the healing process.

During the first four nights at home the inability to sleep was a constant companion. On those first four nights the sun came up before I was able to sleep. My mother contacted Dr. Frank who prescribed a sleep aid. The first night of sleep was a much welcome change.

The day I was transferred from Memphis to the Magnolia Hospital in Corinth, Dr. Wood gave orders that whenever I was discharged from the Magnolia, I was not to drive an automobile, go to school or work until an electroencephalo-graph (EEG) gave him the results he required.

An EEG is the neurophysiological measurement of the electrical activity of the brain by recordings from electrodes placed on the scalp. It is used to measure comparison of brain activity. It was my displeasure to learn firsthand these electrodes are placed on the scalp with a substance that takes *elbow grease* to remove.

My first follow-up with Dr. Wood was August 28, 1972. As to be expected, the first thing to greet me at the Semmes-Murphy Clinic was an EEG. As I lay down on a table, the electrodes were applied to my scalp using the substance described earlier. By now I was blessed with hair. My hair and the substance were not a match-made-in-Heaven. The EEG would take about 40 minutes. The patient must lie completely still. At one point my teeth lightly touched together. The pretty technician responded, *Don't let your teeth touch.*

I thought, *Wow! This thing can let her know if my teeth touch. Oh my gosh! Can this pretty lady look at the graph and read my thoughts?! Holy Mackerel! I better not think of a girl!*

That may seem funny or silly, but for an 18-year old boy to go 40 minutes without thinking of a girl can be an enormous task. After the EEG was finished and my hair was covered in gunk, the technician told me to go back to the waiting room. Later, my name was called and a meeting with Dr. Wood was near. My thoughts, *Oh please, let the EEG give him the results he wants.* This would allow me to drive and go to school; even though in the back of my mind I knew my poor short-term memory was not ready for college.

Dr. Wood came in the examining room. It was good to see him. He was carrying a blue tobacco pipe; even though it was not lit. He was known for his humor. He had read the results from the EEG. He went on to explain that I still could not go to school, drive a car or work, yet. There were a couple of things he said that made me feel like my recovery was coming along well. He asked if I had experienced any seizures or blackouts.

I replied, *No*, to both.

Dr. Wood explained that those two are very common following a brain injury. That gave me the feeling that my recovery was coming along better than most. I never had anything that even resembled a seizure or blackout. Well, stay tuned. He did tell me that he had never had a patient progress as quickly as I had and for me to be patient. Patience can be difficult for an 18 year-old boy.

My brothers did what they could to make my *new life* as pleasurable as possible. My Mom drove me to Louisiana to visit my brother Ray, his wife Vicki and my nephew Fred. Ray took all of us to New Orleans to the French Quarter. Now, I have been to the French Quarter many times, but after spending 40 nights in a hospital, that was an extra special visit.

My brother, Tom, in early September of 1972 took me to an exhibition football game in Memphis. The Pittsburgh Steelers defeated the New Orleans Saints 63-7. That was during the Saints' early days when trying to cut cost, they had not yet invested in an offensive line. All of Archie's passes were thrown while he was being chased for his life.

By September most of my high school classmates were preparing for their college careers. Some were going to a nearby community college, NEMCC, only 20 miles from my hometown. Many were leaving town and going to 4-year colleges. Not me. I couldn't drive. If I wanted to go anywhere, my mother or father took me in their car. Besides, I knew I couldn't go back to school.

My short-term memory was terrible. Some days it was worse. I would sit down for dinner and could not remember if I had eaten lunch. However, the scent of my hospital room in Memphis was still vivid in my memory . . . and would be for a few years.

My friends had left for college. I didn't want to be left behind. So, taking a correspondence course seemed to be an answer. Just two months earlier I was taking Western Civilization at NEMCC. That was a required course regardless of what 4-year college loomed in my future.

So, taking a correspondence course in Western Civilization from the University of Southern Mississippi (USM) would assist in getting me *back to normal*. A rude awakening was around the corner. With the correspondence course came a text book, which you would expect, and lesson plans. The student was expected to read a section in the book and then complete the lesson plan. The rude awakening occurred with the easy part, reading the book. I would read a paragraph in the text book and by the time the end of the paragraph arrived, I had no idea what was in the first part of the paragraph. It is important for me to emphasize *paragraph*, not page. The correspondence course was returned for a refund.

I knew I was *different*. Even though a little gain in weight had been a much needed addition to my life, my speech impediment was worse than prior to the accident. Also, along with the speech impediment was a new problem with word finding. I could see a chair and hear in my mind the word, *chair*, but how to make my mouth move to say that word was not as easy. Usually, in a few seconds the word would come. I was later to learn this is very common following TBI.

Also, worse than that was a new problem with my short-term memory. I was saying or doing things on impulse that I would not have done only a few months earlier. These were small things, such as outbursts in a social situation that I might not have said earlier or laughing uncontrollably at the smallest thing. My bruised brain was still a bruised brain. It takes time for a bruise to heal. Because my brain is hidden away in my skull, the damage was not visible.

The strength in my left-arm was coming back and I appeared to look as I did prior to the accident. That was to everyone but me; however, it was impossible for me to explain how I felt. Years later I was to learn that the reason I was unable to explain how I felt was due to the fact the very *thing* I use to explain anything, *my brain*, was broken.

That first fall season was slow for me. Although my friends took me to ballgames, and my parents worked diligently to provide me as active a life as possible, it was easy to be bored. I had many people who told me that they had prayed for me or had requested that their church pray for me. I thought, *Well, I guess I'm quite popular.*

Living in a small town and unable to go to school, work or drive a car, things to occupy the mind can be hard to find. One day I did something that I'd not done in a very long time. I was in my bedroom sitting in my mother's mahogany rocking chair and began reading the Bible. Then it hit me. Why me? If God was so good, why did He let this happen to me?

It is important to know that I did realize there were/are millions of people in much worse condition(s) than mine, but for that moment the subject was me. Although I was reading the Bible, I began to doubt God. I realize God owes me nothing. He's never been in debt to me and I don't foresee that changing. Still, I thought if God is all loving, why did He let this happen to me? Consequently, I said this prayer, *God, if You're real, show me.*

I didn't hear a voice or see a vision, but I immediately *felt* a voice say, *Greg, if I'm not real, then who are you talking to?*

RESEMBLANCE OF NORMALCY

READING BECAME EASIER. As time passed I could read a page in a book and as I read the bottom of the page, I could remember what was in the first section. My bruised brain was healing. My weight was slowing increasing. Still, something just wasn't quite right. I no longer *looked* damaged but I knew some things were still different.

Stress issues would visit me on a daily basis. Although not knowing specifically how to label it at the time, problems with impulse control were beginning to be a problem. I would learn later that part had to do with the inability to size-up social situations. This will be discussed in-depth a little later. Also, to compound problems, my speech was still worse than prior to the accident.

December 13, 1972 was my next follow-up with Dr. Wood in Memphis. Naturally, this meant another EEG. After the EEG, I was returned to the waiting room with that gunk in my hair, even though the technician did try to remove as much of it as possible. This time my stay with my parents in the waiting room was 4 hours 45 minutes. Dr. Wood had been called into surgery.

I suppose the need to perform emergency surgery on someone's brain supersedes my need to learn the results of my EEG. Finally, it was my time to see him. He informed me that the results from the EEG would allow me to now drive a car, go to school or work. He again asked me if I had had any seizures or blackouts. Again, the answers were, *No.*

My thoughts – *I had not had any seizures by now. I'm home free.*

As stated earlier, *Stay tuned.* Dr. Wood smiled and told me that I was going *to be fine.*

That was reassuring for the moment. It would be years later that I would wonder why he didn't say, *Now you have to live with it.*

After experiencing seizures, anxiety, depression, short-term memory loss, impulse control problems and other daily consequences of TBI, I would later ask my neurologist why my neurosurgeon would tell me that I'm going to be fine. My neurologist informed me that for a patient who has experienced skull fractures and a bruised brain to be able to get out of bed and walk, in the eyes of a neurosurgeon, that patient has come eons.

It had been 6 months since I had been able to drive. The inability to drive for a now 18 year-old can really limit social outlets, such as dating. A week later, my Dad and I returned to Memphis in search of a used automobile. A used Malibu would do nicely. *Freedom!* I could now date and drive to wherever my heart desired.

A week or so later I had my first date since the accident. It was with a lovely girl, whom I had dated once before my senior year. We went to a drive-in movie, which in my little hometown was about all there was to do. I can remember sitting in my *new* used car and thinking, *Did I have lunch today?*

My first few attempts at dating after being discharged from the hospital did not go too well. The combination of a poor short-term memory, poor impulse control, inability to size-up social situations, along with a worsened speech impediment, did not make me the most appealing person with whom to spend an evening.

The next few months found me staying at home much of the time and going to sporting events whenever possible with the same friends as I had before the accident. I went with them to ballgames and was beginning to date a little. However, in all of those things mentioned, one thing was different. Every night when I came home, no matter what time it was, my mother would be sitting in the den at the end of the couch under a light reading her Bible. She never wavered. Regardless of what time I got home, she never asked where I had been, not that there was a great deal of trouble available in my hometown. She just smiled, closed her Bible and went to bed.

Years later I would work in a facility serving individuals with psychiatric disorders, as well as individuals with chemical dependency. During those years I had the privilege of attending numerous sessions on *Spirituality* presented to the patients by Dr. Bill Spears. He would explain that spirituality is the connection or relationship we have to others, nature, ourselves and God — as we understand God.

When we have that connection we feel hope and worth. Something can come along and cause a gap between others, nature, ourselves and God; consequently, we feel hope-less than we did before the gap or worth-less than we did before the gap. Often, a gap in any of the four mentioned areas will cause gaps in all four. Some of the things that can cause a large gap are illness, divorce, losing a job, family problems or a death. Dr. Spears would then ask, *How can you have a spiritual awakening?* As he asked the question, he would write, *HOW*, on the board. He then explained that you can have a spiritual awakening by being honest, open and willing. Reading the Bible gave to my mother that hope and worth. She was already open to it.

This reading is not an attempt to evangelize anyone. Everyone is entitled to his or her spiritual belief or the lack thereof. However, I do agree with C.W. Metcalf, who said in one of his seminars, *I don't care if you are a Baptist, Buddhist or Agnostic, but I do hope you believe in something greater than yourself, because if you look in the mirror and say to yourself, 'This is as good as it is going to get,' then you're in deep trouble.*

My speech, as it always did, controlled me. To say it was frustrating would not give it justice. I learned of a rehab facility in Tupelo, which is 50 miles from my hometown, where I could receive speech therapy. So, once a week I drove to Tupelo, and for the next few months, received speech therapy. This resulted in very little progress. Focusing and the ability to remember any recent event were a never-ending battle.

By the time summer arrived I was involved in many church activities. This involved playing church league softball. Along with playing softball, I was coaching the same little league team as in 1972, the Crackers, at the YMCA. One afternoon I had taken my then six-year-old nephew, Fred, to the YMCA to throw the baseball with him.

While we were preparing to leave the field, John, a friend from my church came to the nearby fence to speak with me. Fred and I were about to end our pitching and fielding and met John at the fence. John was three years my senior and was very much a leader in the young adult activities at our church. Knowing what I had been through with my auto accident, he said words that sent chills down my spine. He said, *Greg, I was wondering if you would give the opening message at our Sunday School Department on Sunday?*

I immediately thought, *I would much rather face a firing squad!* My fear at that time of speaking in public — any public — was more than most people could fathom. Stress engulfed my body. My response was, *John, not me.*

I held onto the fence and put my head on to the top bar and said, *Oh man, I just don't know. Not me.*

He then uttered words I will never forget, *Well, if you're ashamed of Him, don't do it.*

Hearing those words, I raised my head and said, *I'll do it.*

As the last sound of those words exited my mouth, I felt a burden lifted from my shoulders, which is difficult to describe. Peace and calm was not what I expected, but that is exactly what I experienced at that moment.

The next few days I prepared a testimony, which was a totally new experience for me. Our Sunday School Department was about 45 people from ages 21-29. It might as well been Madison Square Garden — packed.

Sunday morning I met John prior to the meeting. We went to a nearby room to pray one last time before I faced many faces probably shocked to see this young man with a speech impediment offering his testimony. After we prayed, John looked at me and spoke with a caring and sincere expression, *Greg, I want you to go out there and be cool, calm and collected. Please Greg, whatever you do. . . don't start cussing.*

What?! I said, John, *I'm not going to cuss!*

Again, he said, *Greg, don't cuss.*

John was using unexpected humor to calm any remaining jitters. We went to the assembly room. John stood in front of the department, while I sat on the front row feeling very confident. I felt I would was going to get through this with a minimal amount of dysfluency. John made a few announcements and said, *Now, before we dismiss to our classes, Greg Little has a few things he wants to share with you.*

I then stepped to the podium and faced the department. After a brief pause, my mouth opened and I began to speak. Fluently. Completely fluent. Here I was speaking to about 45 people, most of whom were older than me, and I was speaking with no hesitation. No flaws. I stood before those people thinking, *How is this coming out of my mouth?*

I found myself not wanting to stop, but I did have to stop. Afterwards, people came to me and told me how much they enjoyed what I had to say. We went to our classrooms. As we took our chairs, I was feeling very confident. Then I began to speak. . . and stutter. That was a not an issue. I had asked God to speak through me as I was giving my testimony, and He delivered. His part was done, but His part provided a rush I will never forget.

Autumn and the possibility of beginning of a new school year were approaching. What's a fellow to do? After what I had experienced during the past year, the thought of majoring in Law Enforcement no longer had an appeal to me. My initial thought of going to school at USM, which was 285 miles from home, also was not as tempting as it once was.

Having received physical therapy (PT) at the Baptist Hospital was a strong influence for me to go into that field. However, an inquiry of admissions into PT schools revealed a heavy emphasis in science and math; unfortunately, my high school background in those two areas was poor at best.

My older brothers graduated with degrees in Business. Consequently, General Business should work for me. It sure is nice to be a free thinker. There is a state college only 110 miles from home; consequently, the fall of 1973 I enrolled at MS State University with the intent of majoring in Business. Not to offend anyone with a business background, but the only reason I was pursing a business degree was because I had no idea what to do with my life. As mentioned earlier, anxiety and depression following TBI are almost a universal aftermath.

Entering college can be stressful. My stress was compounded with anxiety/depression caused by a physical ailment, along with a severe stutter; even though I will learn years later that I did not actually stutter.

Difficulty paying attention in class and remembering what was being discussed in class resulted in poor grades. The first year in college passed by with an uncertainty of what I wanted to do with my life. Late in the spring of my freshman year, I learned there was to be an opening for a physical therapy aide at the Magnolia Hospital.

A year after my discharge as a patient, the hospital hired its first physical therapist. One PT aide had been hired, but they were in need of another one for the summer. So, at 19 I had my first job in the health care field. This was in 1974, and minimum wage was $2.00 per hour; however, a hospital was considered a non-profit organization. Consequently, my salary was $1.90 per hour.

From what I experienced that summer, the salary was just icing on the cake. The physical therapist taught me how to implement intermittent and pelvic traction, as well as hot pack, ultrasound and massage. My experience as a patient two years earlier allowed me to relate to several of the patients that summer.

That experience grounded my desire to work in the health care field even more so than in the past. Unfortunately, I had no clue as to what health care field to pursue, my second year in college saw me again taking my core courses and preparing for a career in business. Struggling with the same issues, that year was rather uneventful. That was about to change.

There were two nice fellows, who roomed together in the apartment complex where I lived. One, Royce, was majoring in Business Administration as I was. The other, Ben, majored in Recreation. We were shooting basketball one day when I told Ben about my previous aspiration of majoring in Recreation. He then learned of my automobile accident, which led to my inquiries of physical therapy school. Ben said the words that would ultimately alter my life, *USM offers a degree in therapeutic recreation.*

I could pursue a degree which would allow me to work in recreation in the health care field. Oh, this was too good to be true, but it was true.

The following fall I enrolled at USM and completed an undergraduate degree in therapeutic recreation (TR) in 1977. During my senior year, I worked five mornings per week at the local Head Start. My duties were to work exclusively with children with severe challenges.

Working with one seven year-old female in particular, I was able to learn more practical knowledge than any book could possibly teach. She was born with no complications. At 11-months of age she developed meningitis, which caused a very high fever resulting in a lack of oxygen to the brain, anoxia. The anoxia resulted in her becoming quadriplegic, as well as profoundly retarded. She lay at home for the next six years. Her muscles atrophied from the lack of use/stimulation.

The first day this young lady and I met she could not hold up her head, her fingers were in fists, her extremities were very rigid, and she was totally non-verbal.

My mornings always began with getting her to smile. Afterwards, I worked on her neck, fingers, hands, arms, and every digit and joint in her body. When I graduated the next

May, she was able to hold-up her head, her hands were no longer in fists and, most of all, her quality of life had improved. All these things would never have been possible if I had not had my automobile accident, been in a coma and had to relearn to walk. All the things she was able to do gave me a rush.

Also during my senior year, as my instructor, who was also advisor, was walking down the aisles returning test papers to the class, he handed mine to me and said, *Stop by my office when you have time.*

I looked at my test score. It was in the 90's, not bad. What could he want to tell me that would warrant my going to his office? He never said this to any of the other students. After the class ended and after my instructor walked to his office, I followed a few minutes behind. When I got to his office, he offered me a chair, which I accepted. He then told me that working in therapeutic recreation will at times require me to speak to groups. He mentioned that the speech therapy department at the university offered therapy for students. When he heard that I was already utilizing their services, he smiled and said, *Oh, good.*

That was good. The bad part was that he had not noticed my speech had improved. That was because my speech had not improved. Graduate students were conducting the therapy. It would be years before I went to a speech therapist, which would make an impact on me. Perhaps that last sentence should be rephrased, *A speech therapist, who I would allow to be an impact on me.*

When in college, I was looking for a speech therapist to *fix me.* It was not until learning that was not going to happen, and realizing that the work must be done by the client that I was empowered.

A degree in Therapeutic Recreation requires an internship. My internship was during a summer semester at a governmental hospital. About a year following my MVA I began learning American Sign Language used by people who are deaf. My interest in this was due to my understanding firsthand the frustration one can have by not being able to communicate, such as I experienced while I was a patient at the Baptist Hospital.

My sign language pursuit was known by my supervisors at the hospital. This led to my primary supervisor there, while meaning well, to recommend that I pursue employment following college that would allow me to work with the deaf. The reason – I wouldn't have to talk. I considered that, but oh, the doors we often close on ourselves.

My first employment after college was at a large state funded center serving individuals with developmental disabilities. *Developmental disability* is the term now used to refer to people who were once considered to have mental retardation. The center had nine (9) cottages housing individuals with various ranges of developmental disabilities.

One of those buildings was a nursing home serving sixty (60) residents, all of whom were either bed-bound or in wheelchairs. Most of these individuals were unable to speak and were diagnosed with severe/profound mental retardation. I was assigned to work at that building three days a week and with the low-functioning ambulatory residents from other cottages the other two days.

Working one-on-one with each resident at the nursing home, I was able to develop a relationship with each of them. These relationships came through providing range of motion, teaching them to grasp an object, how to respond to massage if they were comatose, as well as other auditory and visual stimulation.

Because I was not a physical therapist, I stated that my range of motion and massage was *tactile stimulation*. The other two days of the week I worked with the low-functioning residents. The great majority were non-verbal.

Since my primary duties were motor skills development for these individuals, one day my supervisor handed an article to me regarding massage therapy being advocated for the profoundly retarded. Since having learned to massage while working at the Magnolia Hospital, this caught my interest. I began taking profoundly retarded children, who were unable to talk, and massage their backs.

During each session the only people in the room were the child, who lay on a mat, his/her special education teacher and me. All of these children were very active. Being still and calm for them was not a normal experience. By the end of their massage with slow long strokes, each child was still. Their teachers were amazed, as was I.

Another time we had children, who were non-verbal and with severe/profound developmental disabilities, to play in whipped cream. They put it on themselves, the teachers and me. They were having a new experience . . . fun with one another. Working at the center conveyed to me that perhaps I had found my niche in life . . . as least one of them.

I still had not overcome any adversity in my eyes. That would later prove to be a wrong assumption. Impulse control issues, specifically doing or saying something that would later cause me to want to kick myself, were still constant concerns.

Years later I would realize that if you want to be good in something, make sure it is something you know very well. If one wants to overcome an adversity, do just that; know all you can about that adversity. Most of the time, no one is as good at something as those who have lived it.

The first day of my four years spent working with individuals with chemical dependency began with a group called *community*. It involves all patients and staff meeting for an hour discussion much like AA. There were eleven (11) staff members present. I was the only one not in recovery for drug or alcohol addiction.

Years later, while working in another facility for individuals with chemical dependency and leading another community session, a male client stated he did not believe he could learn much from someone who had not *walked in his shoes*. He meant that because I was not an addict, how could I teach him not to use drugs? This is often typical of individuals receiving in-patient treatment for drug addiction.

It is very rare for these individuals to come to treatment to get off of drugs. They primarily come to treatment to prevent them from having to go to jail, losing a job, losing a marriage, or to say to their family, *See, I told you it was not going to work.*

To reply to this man's question, my statement to the group was, *If you need someone to tell you how to use cocaine, crystal meth or IV drugs, I am not your man, but if you need someone to teach you how to be live sober, I have more experience than anyone in the room.*

There are exceptions. Neither of the two physicians who delivered my two sons into the world has ever given birth. Nice fellows, though.

The next year I accepted a position as Therapeutic Recreation Director at another center serving individuals with developmental disabilities on the Gulf Coast. While living on the Coast, I was, as usual, everyone's comic relief.

Glen Thaxton, a nice fellow I had met in my apartment complex, had heard my impersonations – often. There was going to be a talent contest at a nearby lounge. First place was to win $50, which in 1979 was not bad. After much persuasion Glen finally convinced me to register for the contest. After developing my impersonation of The Ed Sullivan Show and some feedback from Glen, I was ready. Glen would repeatedly say, *Greg, that $50 is in your hand.*

The time came. With the encouragement from Glen and knowing the impersonations were rather good, I confidentially went to the stage. There were about seven (7) acts that night. Mine was one of the first and included impersonations of Ed Sullivan, Marlon Brando as The Godfather, James Cagney, Walter Brennan, a fly (couldn't resist that one), a Sears Catalog, Elvis Presley and Arnold Schwarzenegger.

After my act, it was evident from the feedback of the audience that my act was well received, and yes, I did win. One thing that was implanted in my memory was that while I was doing the impersonations, I never stuttered. The reason for this would be realized years later in speech therapy.

IT CANNOT BE CURED
... BUT

IN 1982 I had been working for two (2) years as a unit director at another center serving individuals with developmental disabilities. One of my duties was to chair a team meeting once each week for about an hour. So, picture a man with a speech impediment chairing a meeting for an hour. Hold that thought.

Because my position required that I supervise people and chair meetings, the ability to verbally convey my thoughts, information and directives was obviously a very significant aspect of the job. For two (2) years the individuals I supervised, as well as my co-workers, had to listen carefully to understand my speech. Years later I would relate to what a speech therapist would say, *When you have a speech impediment, it lowers people's expectations of you.*

Someone at the facility informed me that because my speech was related to my employment, Mississippi Vocational Rehabilitation might pay for me to receive speech therapy. Upon contacting Vocational Rehab this belief was confirmed.

I was approved to receive speech therapy for one-hour sessions, every week for one-year. An appointment was made for me to be assessed and then receive speech therapy at the University Medical Center (UMC) in Jackson.

The day of my assessment I met Judson Farmer, who was my assigned Speech Therapist. The initial meeting began with Mr. Farmer saying, *During this first session, I will do most of the talking. During all of the remaining sessions, you will do most of the talking.*

He explained a few of the logistics and instructed me to read a passage, which he recorded. Afterwards, he said to me, *I can detect a slight form of dysarthria in your speech. Have you ever had a head injury?*

Wow! He knew nothing of my history; yet, could detect from my speech that I had previously had a head trauma.

I replied, *Yes.*

He said, *I thought so.*

I knew then that I had been assigned to the speech therapist from whom I would gain the most benefit. He then said, *Listening to your speech, I have determined that you don't stutter. What you do is clutter, meaning you talk too fast. It cannot be cured, but it can be controlled.*

He then gave to me the six-rules of good speech. These six-rules, though they might seem obvious, opened a new world to me:

1) Think – about what you say before you say it.
2) Breathe – talk as you exhale, rather than inhale. That may seem simple, but people with speech impediments at time attempt to speak when they inhale rather than when they exhale.
3) Move your mouth. This is important for articulation.
4) Make all sounds. It is not uncommon for one to drop the last sound of a word.
5) Use enough voice.
6) Talk slowly – in order for it to sound normal to the listener, it must sound abnormal to me.

The first five rules are for everyone. Number 6, is for those with a speech impediment. Mr. Farmer gave those rules to me, and I left the first session.

My treatment team meeting was the following morning. Here it goes. I used those 6-rules of good speech, and the treatment team members were stunned. A few came to me following the meeting to tell me how they noticed a drastic change in my speech. Some actually believed I was *cured*. Be assured I'm not. Only by using the tools given to me by professionals can my speech impediment, my *adversity* if you please, be controlled.

For the next year I met weekly with Mr. Farmer, and my speech was noticeably improving. The last day of my speech therapy, he asked me to read a passage. The passage was read with me knowing it sounded good even by his expectations. After I confidently put the passage aside, Mr. Farmer said, *Now, I want you to listen to this.*

He then pushed a button on a tape recorder. It was then that I heard the most horrific attempt by anyone to speak. It was obviously a young man or teenager, possibly crippled with cerebral palsy, attempting to read the same passage that I had just read. When he finished, I said, *My gosh! Who was that?!*

His next words I will never forget. He said, *That was you, on your first day of therapy.*

More speech therapy and speaking instruction would follow in the coming years. However, the primary lesson learned from this experience, as well as others that you will read about later, was that people who face adversity are limited – only by their ability to adapt. Using the tools given to me by Mr. Farmer allowed me to adapt my speech . . . quite nicely.

SPEAKING IN PUBLIC –
OR, WOULD YOU RATHER EAT RAZOR BLADES?

IN THE MID-1980'S I was offered a position with the agency assigned by the State Department of Health to inspect hospitals, nursing homes, as well as intermediate care facilities for the mentally retarded (ICF's/MR) in Mississippi. My responsibilities were to inspect four disciplines: patient activities, social services, patient rights and discharge planning. One aspect of the position involved speaking during preceptor workshops.

Frankly, I had no idea what a preceptor was. I would later learn that a preceptor in nursing home settings is an individual who is authorized to train a Nursing Home Administrator-in-training. Every few weeks, preceptor training was scheduled, usually in Jackson. I was assigned to teach the preceptors about my four disciplines.

How was I going to get through this? Why, employ a little humor of course. After developing the information my audience needed to hear, I would sprinkle humor throughout each presentation. This would come via a joke, audience interaction or, the best one, making fun of myself whenever making a mistake. The audience would laugh, which obviously made them feel good.

They were laughing, because of something I had said or done. When we laugh, we purge our stress. The brain releases endorphins, which provides us a clean high. Consequently, they liked me for assisting them in obtaining this clean high. Ultimately, we had a bond, and they liked me. By controlling when they received this jolt of endorphins, I was in charge and spoke with confidence.

This was a new experience for me. My confidence level shot skyward; therefore, when speaking in public my dysfluency was greatly decreased. Nursing home administrators were contacting my supervisor and requesting that I speak at their facility or at a conference. While speaking to these groups, I learned to utilize something that I had learned from Mr. Farmer during one of my speech therapy sessions — Delayed Auditory Feedback.

One day he had me wear headphones and read into a microphone. This apparatus allowed him to control how fast my spoken words went back into the headphones, which meant he would control how fast I would hear myself talk. He totally controlled how fast – or more importantly how slow – I read the passage. He was having fun. This was obvious by his giggling as my rate of reading the passage was altered by his turn of the knob.

That experience taught me to always test the microphone before my audience came into the room. While speaking into the microphone, I would tell the audio/visual professional to *turn it up*.

I continued to tell him/her to do so until I got the auditory feedback, with which I am comfortable. What am I doing? I'm just practicing my ability to adapt or . . . overcoming an adversity.

In the fall of 1984 I had a birdbrain idea. By now my confidence regarding speaking in public was beginning to improve; though I would learn years later that it would improve a great deal more. Anyway, I thought that in order to assist Activity Directors in my state to develop workable care plans for their residents; I could conduct a six-hour workshop. My supervisors with the state licensure agency thought that would be a good idea.

We could conduct it at the Research & Development (R&D) Center in Jackson, which seats 187. People could come from all over the state, and we would have as much *hands-on* learning as possible. The secretarial staff at the office did an incredible job. Handouts were developed for each participant. All 187 seats were filled. I invested weeks – make that months – developing that rascal.

During that time I developed activities for individuals who are bedridden or comatose, as well as pet therapy, activities just for men and non-competitive group games. With regard to providing therapeutic activities to comatose individuals, I recommended putting an earplug in one of their ears and playing music from their youth.

They probably will not hear music coming from a radio on the nightstand but might hear music coming from an earplug. I was going to use as much audience participation as possible.

I had read somewhere that if you tell someone something, they forget it. If you show someone something, they remember it for a little while. However, if they do it, it becomes a part of them. Then, it happened. The night before the workshop, a little voice in my head said, *What in the Sam Hill are you doing?!*

The workshop went off without a glitch. The majority of my program involved participants coming to the stage and doing the activities. This allowed them to experience the activities their residents would be experiencing. I used the microphone which provided the delayed auditory feedback; consequently, I spoke fluently. However, much of my fluency, I believe, was due to me focusing more on my topic than my speech.

Years later I would be in a support group for people who stutter. The group was chaired by Dr. Bob Rhodes, who I mentioned earlier. It was then that Dr. Rhodes made the comment, *Stuttering is something people, who stutter, do when they try not to stutter.*

Dr. Rhodes was right. During the workshop, I was as animated as possible . . . yes, I hammed it up. It ended with my first standing ovation. THAT was a rush!

The following year I did the same. My office supported me in presenting another six-hour workshop at the R&D Center. Though this workshop had a great deal of different material from the previous one, it did not take as long to develop. I would realize years later that all of the programs I have led since that time have been spin-offs of the first one I conducted in 1984.

Granted, the topic or material for a specific seminar may have nothing to do with that initial one, but everything was somehow related to my first one. Yet, much of my material had been spin-offs from spin-offs. Following one of my early seminars, a social worker came to me while I has gathering my material from the stage, and said, *Greg, our physician wanted me to thank you. We took your advice and put an earplug in Mr. Smith's ear, and he came out of his coma.*

I'm not going to say that putting an earplug in his ear brought him out of his coma. However, the social worker's words did provide me with a positive feeling.

Hundreds learn more about mental health

BY MICHAELA GIBSON MORRIS
Daily Journal

TUPELO – More than 600 people gathered Friday to laugh a little and also learn about mental health.

Professionals and consumers sat side by side at the North Mississippi Mental Health Community Conference at the Ramada Inn Convention Center.

"It's a really unique experience," said Aurora Baugh of the state Department of Mental Health, which sponsored the conference. "We've got a little bit of everything."

Seminars covered the use of humor, holistic approaches to wellness, team building, depression, case management, schizophrenia medication, drug addiction, disability benefits, exercise and conflict resolution.

Patricia Carter of Ackerman, who has attended a previous state conference, said she was enjoying it.

"I've learned a lot both years," she said.

"Consumers attending the conference paid only $1; the rest of the cost is covered by the mental health department," Baugh said.

In past years, a single statewide conference has been held in Jackson. This year the department is hosting regional conferences in Tupelo, Jackson and Hattiesburg to make the programs more accessible to more people, Baugh said.

"It saves on expenses" connected with travel and overnight hotels, said Drue Sutherland, executive director of Region III Mental Health in Tupelo.

Community Counseling in Starkville brought the largest group with nearly 250 attendees.

"By separating [the regional conferences], I think the consumers will get more out of it," said Jackie Edwards, executive director of Community Counseling.

Greg Little, of the Mississippi State Hospital, goes through a memory exercise with the audience during his presentation on "Laughter: A Serious Medicine" during the North Mississippi Mental Health Community Conference in Tupelo on Friday.

Perhaps you are wondering how someone with a short-term memory problem could conduct a 6-hour workshop. How could I know what I was going to say or keep track of the material? Initially, I used an overhead projector. It is very important to know that I did not put all the material to be discussed on the transparencies and read to my audience. That would have been rude. It unnerves me to attend a seminar and have the presenter read to me. I can read just fine at home. If someone is going to read to me, would it not be better if he would save me a trip and just mail the material to me?

For each activity, and there were more than 100 presented, by using a piece of typing paper to cover the transparent paper, I uncovered the name of the activity, which was often one word. Afterwards, I would walk across the stage and talk about the activity or, more often, *choose* attendees (my drafted volunteers) from the audience and conduct the activity. This allowed me to control the pace of the seminar and allow the participants to write their own description of the activity. Also, people taking notes required me to pace my delivery.

If you are contemplating conducting seminars, go for it! Those who can speak in front of a group have a *leg-up* on everyone else. Any beginning speaker should try to cover all the things that may go wrong. What if someone in the audience asks a question and you don't know the answer? *Ooh . . . that is going to happen.* Unless you can wing-it pretty good, I would like to suggest trying this: *That's a good question. Has anyone in the room had the same problem or can help her with this?*

Don't worry. People will respond to that. Professionals like to share their success stories . . . and they should.

A great deal of confidence to speak in public came from the year of speech therapy given to me by Justin Farmer. Remember rule #5, which was *use enough voice*? All of those six rules are important.

Not using any one rule is like missing a link in a chain . . . the chain does not work. Using enough voice is vital.

The best example of doing so is the Mississippi-born actor, James Earl Jones. He possesses perhaps the best known voice in all of Hollywood. He was the voice of Darth Vader in *Star Wars* and his beautiful full voice was well-known from his role in *Field of Dreams*. At a very early age, Jones developed a stutter so severe he refused to speak aloud.

When he moved to Brethren, Michigan in later years a teacher at the Brethren schools started to help him with his stutter. He remained functionally mute for eight years until he reached high school. He credits a high school teacher, who discovered he had a gift for writing poetry, with helping him out of his silence. The teacher believed forced public speaking would help him gain confidence and insisted he recite a poem in class each day. Jones would later state that he was someone who stuttered and couldn't talk. His first year of school was his first year as a mute. Those mute years continued until he got to high school. Hence, he developed a full voice.

The hardest part for me would ultimately be what Mr. Farmer said would be the most difficult part . . . *in order for it to sound normal to the listener - it must sound abnormal to me.*

I was accustomed to speaking at a very fast pace essentially all of my life. That rapid speech became my norm. Hearing calm articulate speech coming from my lips seemed odd. It had to become a constant.

My speech impediment is not cured; nor will it ever be cured. However, it can be controlled as long as I employ the 6-rules of good speech. It does not always work. Oh, allow me to correct that. I don't always work it.

When my speech would get to be so dysfluent to the point it was unnerving to me, I went back to the support group, which was a controlled environment. It would give me the opportunity to speak fluently . . . one might say, *a booster shot.*

Strange as it may seem, it is not easy. My current employment is that of an alcohol & drug (A&D) therapist. We use the 12-steps of Alcoholics Anonymous (AA). My clients' disease of chemical dependency cannot be cured; however, if they work the 12-steps of AA and bond with a support group along with a couple of other things, they can live a clean sober life. If they fail to practice even one of the 12-steps, sobriety is essentially futile. If I do not practice all of my 6-rules, speaking fluently for me is essentially futile.

A few years later I was employed as a counselor at a private facility treating clients with mental illness. The director of the center, Dr. Bill Osborne, had the clearest articulated speech I had ever heard. His enunciation was down to an art form. Frankly, I was in awe of his speech. I mentioned to him that I stuttered. I rarely state, *cluttering*, because most people have never heard of cluttering. His next words I will never forget. After I told him that I stutter, he replied, *I do too*.

Could he be patronizing me? No, he was serious. He told me that he was able to control his speech on his own. He emphasizes the last sound of each word. Try it. You may impress yourself.

One day while sitting in a circle in community session in a facility treating individuals with chemical dependencies, one of the counselors, Paul Berry, was sitting next to me. Paul had begun reading an article aloud to the patients. Naturally, it was an article focusing on addiction, which is a terminal illness. Consequently, any tidbit we could give them that might reach one of them was worth a try. Shortly after Paul began reading the article, he was paged over the intercom to come to the front office, Paul got up from his chair, placed the article in my lap and said, *Read this, Greg*.

Paul immediately left the room. Here I was sitting in a circle with 30-40 sets of eyes looking at me. We had admitted new patients the previous couple of days; consequently, not everyone there had met me. How was I to get through this? It was totally impromptu and it had provided me no time to scan the article for any words that would be difficult for me to pronounce. All there was for me to think, *Dr. Osborne, I hope you are right*.

Reading the article and emphasizing the last sound of each word left me in awe of what was coming from my mouth. My delivery was 100% fluent. Upon completing the article, a lady who had never met me and sitting about twelve seats to my right said, *You are a very good reader*.

What a rush! Her words will be stored in my memory bank until the day I leave this planet.

You have read how my speech impediment was addressed by Mr. Farmer, then by Dr. Osborne. I stated that if I did not practice all 6-rules given by Mr. Farmer, speaking fluently would be futile. Could this be a contrast from Dr. Osborne's advice to emphasize the last sound of each word? Not really. All Dr. Osborne was doing was emphasizing rule #4 given to me by Mr. Farmer. That rule was, *Make all sounds*.

LIKE A BOULDER HITTING A CALM LAKE

IN THE SPRING of 1984, while attending a therapeutic recreation seminar, I met a lovely young lady, Pam. We began dating in the summer and were married the next year. Later that year, we decided it was time to move from my apartment into a house. November of that year, we found a cute little home in a nice neighborhood. It even had a fireplace. So, we made an offer and that night signed the papers. During that night something happened that until then, I had not experienced.

About 2:00 AM my wife awoke to see me shaking as if I was receiving electrical shocks. My arms and legs were straight out and rigid and violently shaking. I was having a seizure. It was my first one, and it was a grand mal seizure.

When it was over, I lay in bed and slept. I could hear myself snoring. Every muscle of my body was sore for the next twenty-four hours. A phone call was made to the general practitioner I had been seeing for routine medical issues. He told me over the telephone that I had a hysterical reaction and to just lay off the beer. Hysterical reaction?! I was sound asleep. It did not take long for me to trash his opinion and look for another opinion.

An appointment was made for me to see a neurologist, Dr. Ancel Tipton. He prescribed an anticonvulsant medication. He then proceeded to tell me things I had known for years but had never heard someone tell me. Until then I had no idea other people with TBI faced the same issues. With regard to my TBI, Dr. Tipton said, *You will never be able to take as much as others can. You will always need rest. You will have a hard time coping with stress. You will always be tired at the end of the day.*

The seizure was caused by my TBI; even though my TBI occurred more than 13 years earlier. It was a sobering meeting. He asked about my career aspirations and about my present employment. The anticonvulsant medication worked . . . as long as I took it.

A few months later and after we had moved into our new home, another seizure came calling. Like the previous seizure, it was nocturnal, occurring when I was asleep. Also, like the previous one, it was a grand mal. Another appointment was made with Dr. Tipton. Before I was to meet with him, I was scheduled to have another EEG. Remember those?

They have not changed much. The electrodes are still applied with crazy glue or something close to it. A few days after the EEG, I had an appointment to meet with Dr. Tipton. This time my wife went with me. I had to confess to Dr. Tipton that because I was feeling fine, I was not taking my medication as prescribed. He assured me that I needed to continue taking them. He heard no resistance from me. He then was very frank with me, and his next comments would change my life. He said, *Greg, in the couple of times we've met, you've impressed me as a young man who could do more than you are doing career wise. I would recommend you find another position that is more challenging . . . where you can apply your skills . . . and find something that would be less stressful.*

Being affirmed by an expert in his field is a humbling experience. It also caused me to think about doing just that. It also made me wonder, *How was I to do this?*

October 21, 1987 was the greatest day of my life. At 5:30 p.m. our first son was born. I had the privilege of being present when he arrived into the world. You may think you can prepare yourself for the reality of parenthood, but when it happens, it can be so surreal. To know a human being is entering the world because of your existence is an awesome responsibility.

Requests to speak at symposia, conferences or workshops in-state were coming with greater frequency. Early 1989 found me in Hattiesburg, MS, meeting with Dr. Paul Cotten to discuss a seminar I was preparing. I shared with Dr. Cotten the suggestion from Dr. Tipton to pursue another line of work. Dr. Cotten asked what I would like to do. With my broken speech I timidly told him that I would like to conduct workshops. With a positive aura he said, *Since you want to teach adults in these workshops, why don't you pursue a Ph.D. in Adult Education?* Ooh, this could be my way to pursue Dr. Tipton's suggestion.

The summer of 1989 was the beginning of my work toward a terminal degree in Adult Education. Also, that summer I began my aspirations to speak on a national level. I developed a flier promoting my 6-hour workshop and found the addresses of associations providing long-term health care services in all 50 states. I then mailed letters along with the fliers nationwide.

A couple of weeks passed before receiving the first call. Standing in my study at our home, I heard the lady on the other end tell me that she was the Education Director from a nearby state. She asked how much I charged for my workshop. I told her my fee included my flight, hotel room and meals, and then I mentioned a four-digit amount. She said, *We want a two-day conference. What do you charge for two days?*

I remember closing my eyes and just doubling the previous amount. There was silence on the other end. Oh, no! I'd never done a fee estimate and I've already scared off my first customer!

I said, *Is that ok?*

She replied, *Oh, yes, I'm just making a note of it. I'll mail your plane ticket to you tomorrow.* I hung up the telephone.

That two-day (12-hour) conference was held in July 1989. The response was very positive. Using a microphone, the delayed auditory feedback worked to perfection . . . or close enough. At the end of the second day, I shared with my audience in excess of 100 attendees, that I had a speech impediment. The facial and verbal responses from the entire room conveyed shock and disbelief.

By being able to adapt, I had overcome my adversity. More specifically, by having been shown or having asked someone how to adapt, I had overcome my adversity.

The next year requests to speak nationwide began coming in at a consistent rate. Long-term health care associations in several states have now booked me multiple times. Always using *hands-on* training and incorporating laughter as much as possible, I have realized that people want to laugh. They want to be made to feel important. Also, although my speech imitment cannot be *cured*, I remind myself that I am limited only by my ability to adapt. So are you.

By now you may be puzzled or find it odd that someone with a speech impediment could be a public speaker. Don't feel alone. I am puzzled as well. Then I remembered a statement by a former co-worker. The late Mark Guidry said, *Our weaknesses are our strengths taken to the extreme.*

If someone were to ask me what I consider my strength, I would have to say, *My ability to speak.* If someone were to ask what I consider my weakness, I would reply, *My speech.*

Bit of a contradiction, huh? Not really. Mark's statement was right. My strength, speech, when taken to the extreme, which means speaking too fast, becomes my weakness. I just have to find -- and use -- the means available to me to slow my speech. I also have a new mindset. For the first time in my life, my speech does not control my life. I control it or I let it control me; even though it is not completely cured. Either way, it is my decision.

It takes concentration, as well as an understanding that sometimes I will still fail. A funny thing happens whenever I fail at something; the sun still comes up the next day. I've also learned that failure is an experience – not a person.

THE HUMAN BRAIN – NO COMPUTER CAN COMPARE

BEFORE MOVING TO South Mississippi and pursuing a PhD in Adult Education, I secured employment at a facility serving individuals with psychiatric disorders, as well as individuals with chemical dependency. One day at work I came across excerpts from a book, <u>Traumatic Brain Injury and Neuropsychological Impairment</u> (1990) Springer-Verlag, by Dr. Rolland Parker from New York Medical College. I was awestruck when reading it. It was as if someone had opened my mind and read how I felt and knew the issues I had been facing.

I knew my issues could not be seen; consequently, people think I am *cured*. Dr. Parker's preface included the statement, *The victim's ability to communicate the full quality of their distress is usually not understood. No wonder! The brain, the very organ of experience, communication and understanding has been damaged.*

Later in the preface, Dr. Parker made the comment, *Anxiety and depression become constant companions. The victim soon learns he or she is unable to perform at the level expected . . . .*

I would later undergo a psychological test in which I was diagnosed with anxiety and depression. Those two disorders might seem to be totally different, but rarely does one symptom occur without the other.

I took the excerpts of Dr. Parker's book, which included information on short-term memory and impulse control, home for Pam to read. She said, *Greg, this describes you perfectly.*

There was no other choice but to order the book. I embraced it. Every opportunity was taken for me to know my adversity. It can be said that one's adversity is his enemy. Marlon Brando, playing Don Corleone in The Godfather, said, *Keep your friends close to you, but keep your enemies closer.*

My TBI was my enemy, and I was determined to know all about it. A letter was sent to Dr. Parker congratulating him on the book and telling him how it really *hit home* with me. Surprisingly, he phoned me at home to thank for my statements. We developed a friendship, which grew into our corresponding by mail and telephone.

One day during a telephone conversation, he asked me if I knew the definition of a *mild* brain injury. I did not. He told me it was the kind that happens to the other fellow. He was right. It has been my experience to compare a *mild* brain injury to being a *little* pregnant.

Years later I would move to the Jackson area and attend the Jackson TBI Support Group, which I would eventually chair. Each month we would hear a guest speaker. The information I learned was mind boggling. One area that I had been having trouble with was poor impulse control. By attending the support group, I learned that impulse control is primarily caused by damage to the frontal lobe.

My entire brain was bruised; consequently, the frontal lobe was not spared. Also, the primary thing your brain does is tell you what not to do. When these inhibitors are severed during TBI, one may lose a split second then speak or do something that someone with an undamaged brain would not say or do.

After becoming involved with the TBI support group and working in the mental health field, I made every effort to learn as much about TBI as possible. There was no other way I would know *the enemy* and how to respond to it. Traumatic brain injury or TBI has been mentioned throughout this reading; yet, it has not been defined.

The Brain Injury Society defines traumatic brain injury as *an insult to the brain caused by a direct blow to the skull via a closed or open head injury. Any insult to the brain is referred to as a brain injury. Any problem that affects the brain creates difficulties for the affected individual and their immediate family.*

During my years of involvement in TBI programs and support groups, it has been my experience to meet individuals with an *acquired* brain injury. That is an injury to the brain secondary to trauma, stroke, post-surgical complications, and/or certain disease processes (e.g., tumors, aneurysms). These individuals present many of the same symptoms as those who have experienced a physical insult to the brain, i.e., anxiety/depression and fatigue. However, it has been my experience that short-term memory issues are at times not as prevalent for these individuals compared to individuals, who have experienced TBI due to a direct blow to the head.

Though the majority of individuals I have met with TBI, acquired their injury via a motor vehicle accident, there are multiple ways by which a TBI can occur. Some of these are bullet wounds, physical assaults, physical battering, shaken baby syndrome, domestic violence, falls, as well as sports and recreation injuries. Consequences of TBI may include; cognitive, speech, hearing, taste, smell, balance, vision, physical mobility dysfunctions, and psycho-social, behavioral and/or emotional impairments.

It has been my pleasure to meet two ladies, who each acquired a TBI, which resulted in the loss of their ability to smell. Consequently, it also resulted in the loss of their ability to taste. One lady's TBI occurred when she was involved in a motorcycle accident, while sitting on the back of the motorcycle and wearing a helmet. The other lady fell off a ladder. The one, who fell off the ladder, has problems with word finding, and both have issues with poor impulse control.

Traumatic brain injury is referred in some writings as *The Silent Epidemic*, because it is often unseen. Physical symptoms often do not accompany a brain injury, therefore; the injury is not visible. Consequently, people, often even those in health care professions, will accuse the TBI survivor's symptoms as malingering . . . symptoms by choice rather than due to the actual trauma.

It is my belief this distrust stems from the fact that many health care professionals, with the exception of those in neurology, have virtually no education related to traumatic brain injury during their academic preparation. The great majority of professionals, such as nurses, therapeutic recreation specialist, social services and physical therapist, in mental health have very little, if any, education relative to the consequences of TBI.

There are also injuries that occur to the brain that do not occur from a blow to the head or from a secondary injury. A rapid motion of the head in many directions often referred to as *whiplash* can cause traumatic brain injury. This is the result of an acceleration and deceleration of the head during which the brain is thrust back and forth at crushing speeds thus bouncing the brain off the walls of the skull. The brain becomes injured during the rapid acceleration and deceleration. My injuries came from the direct blows to my head, as well as the rapid acceleration and deceleration of my brain against my skull.

While attending a TBI support group, I met a young man, whose brain injury occurred from none of the examples given earlier. About a year prior to our meeting, he tried to come to the rescue of a young lady, who was being assaulted. In his attempt to intervene, the assailant stabbed the young man, who lost virtually all of his blood. No blood to carry oxygen to the body resulted in anoxia.

The emergency rescue team did an excellent job of getting him to triage, and the surgeons performed the procedures necessary to save his life. Nevertheless, the lack of oxygen which is carried by the blood had done its damage. Today, this young man looks as if nothing is wrong. However, the issues related to anxiety, depression, fatigue, short-term memory and timelines, are constant companions.

Researching the Internet has been helpful in learning about my challenges. However, attending support groups and/or seminars and hearing excellent speakers have proven my best resource. That does not mean it would be the best option for you. We did not all come off of a conveyor belt. It is just that for me to hear someone speak about what I have experienced or am experiencing has been the best outlet for me.

Some of the points I have learned by attending the support groups and seminars are:

- TBI is characteristically a consequence of a frightening experience. Apparently, this is a good reason it is called *traumatic.*
- Inability to deal with change and complexity is universal. Regardless if one has a TBI, the greatest stressor we have in life in change. If one has a TBI and is trying to cope with change, his stress is greatly enhanced. Routine is important. Supervising people can be a very stressful proposition. The TBI survivor should know his limitations and capabilities and work within those boundaries. Large amount of stress can virtually shutdown short-term memory.
- Emotional distress following brain injury is universal. Family members and co-workers should take every step possible to understand that the survivor's brain, which is the CEO of all information in the body, is damaged; consequently, emotional distress is not the fault of the survivor.
- Slow thinking is often characteristic of brain damage. Being pushed to answer rapid-fire questions can cause stress, which has precipitated grand mal seizures.
- The more severe the injury, the greater the possibility of seizures. As stated earlier, my first one did not occur until 13.5 years following my TBI; nevertheless, grand mal seizures can ruin your entire day.
- Headaches are associated with anxiety and depression.
- Inability to learn from experience – a common deficit and is frequently attributed to frontal lobe injury. Many times when someone displays an inappropriate behavior, a friend will inform him that his behavior or spoken words resulted in negative feedback from someone, and that behavior will stop. However, someone

with a TBI might be informed of the negative feedback, yet continue the behavior. This often destroys relationships, because people cannot see that it is a physical problem. It is important for the caregiver to realize that it is not *all or nothing*. You cannot expect the survivor to go to zero outbursts.

- Communication problems are common. Aphasia is most common immediately post-trauma with severe brain damage. Many of my friends with TBI, including myself, have experienced this. Dysarthria is the disorder of the cerebral motor mechanism of speech articulation. As mentioned earlier, Mr. Farmer was able to detect my dysarthria. It is important to know that when you meet someone with a speech impediment and that person has difficulty saying a word, it is routinely best to wait them out. Do not say the word for them. You may think you are helping them, and your intentions might be good, but this just makes them more apprehensive the next time he has to speak.

- Concentration, which is the ability to maintain attention and activity on a task for a useful period of time, while avoiding distractions. This requires filtering out irrelevant stimuli and maintaining incoming selected information.

- Depression and anxiety are not considered a direct response to brain injury, but rather a reaction to the stress or impairment and injury. However, it should be stressed that the depression and anxiety that confronts a survivor of TBI is not the result of not *toughing it out* or *self-will*. It is a consequence of a direct physical insult to the brain.

- Less than 50% return to work.

- There is a much greater probability of divorce following TBI. This is been related to frustration, depression, and social isolation in relation to family adjustment problems following traumatic injury. Relationship breakdowns following brain injury are quite common.

This is not surprising. A spouse marries one person, but following the injury, is married to someone else. All of our feelings, be it erotic and intimate, are manifested in the brain. The longer a couple deals with a brain injury, the more likely the marriage would end.

- Loss of energy can be directly related to brain injury. Rest is extremely important.
- Sleep disorders are common and every effort to control them should be instituted.
- The TBI survivor would do well to keep a notebook for memory. It is not possible to record one's entire day, but appointments and timelines are a good start.
- Support groups! This cannot be emphasized enough.
- Memory. According to Dr. Howard Katz, *memory is so complex that it defies definition.* I agree. It first requires someone to pay attention. There is no part of the brain that is not related to memory. Immediate memory, which is 80% or more of our memory, has to go through one part of the brain stem. If that part is damaged, the person can look normal to you, but cannot remember.
- To put TBI in perspective, one needs to realize that a computer is one billionth or one trillionth of the brain.
- Arthritis is common after TBI. Exercise is good for this.
- Loss of social ability is the incapacity to relate to others at all levels, due to depression, irritability, temper problems, anxiety, social withdrawals, inappropriate jokes, anger and loss of judgment.
- It is assuring for the survivor to be told that his confused state is due to an injury not to an emotional disorder.
- 50-60% of recovery is in the first year. The next 20% is in the second year. The next 20% is the rest of the person's life.

As stated earlier, traumatic brain damage is caused by a frightening experience. Brain damage actually presents a two-fold problem. One, is obvious . . . the brain is damaged. The other is often not as obvious to the layperson. That is, the very organ used for coping . . . with anything . . . including changes, challenges and reactions, is damaged. That organ used for coping is the brain. An individual has experienced damage to the impaired system, as well as damage to the system that is to assist in adjusting to the damage.

An almost universal issue of people with TBI is post-traumatic stress disorder (PTSD). This is often the consequence of a diverse form of anxiety, thoughts that won't go away, constant dwelling on the trauma, denial, being alone, loss of self-worth, feeling like a victim and feeling less attractive due to impairment.

Further, to paraphrase the writing of Dr. Parker (1990), *the victim begins to view the world as dangerous and bleak. He experiences anxiety and depression, inability to enjoy life, social withdrawal, inadequacy and sexual problems.*

All of these problems, in various degrees, have appeared in my life . . . especially the first few years after the accident. Once discharged from the hospital, being approved by my neurosurgeon to drive again after five months post-discharge, gaining a little weight and finally going back to college, it must have seemed to all my friends that the old Greg was back.

Many conversations with survivors of TBI have reinforced the words of Dr. Tipton following my first seizure – *You'll never be able to cope with stress.* Virtually all TBI survivors, whom I have met, face this problem on a daily basis. Many were unable to return to work, due to the stress of coping with the demands and expectations of employment. Often their stress, as in my instance, would initiate seizures.

The consequences become a chain reaction. An anxious situation . . . stress . . . the inability to remember . . . people's disbelief . . . more stress . . . seizures. . . stress . . . These can come in various orders.

The issues TBI survivors confront with short-term memory have been stated. There is not a day that a typical TBI survivor, who has challenges with short-term memory, does not wonder what he will forget that day. This includes the great majority of individuals, who are post-TBI.

The last few pages have described the adversity faced by someone who is challenged by a traumatic brain injury. Now, how does one overcome that adversity? Gene Griessman (1993) Phieffer & Company, <u>The Achievement Factors</u>, states that *high achievers know their strengths and limitations and work within those boundaries.*

Know what you do well . . . and learn to do it better. Research the challenge life has given to you. It may not be a brain injury. It may be a fear of public speaking, a fear of anything. Once your fear becomes the known, it's not so scary.

Have you ever noticed when you are driving your car that everyone else is wrong? Have you ever needed desperately to turn into a lane, and traffic was bumper-to-bumper? All you have to do is look at a driver long enough and he will look at you. Smile. He will always let you in, because you have become the known.

If you say that you've researched and know your challenge, but you have no idea what to do about it. Fine. Then talk to groups about it. Offer it for free at first. In time people will pay you. There are people who will pay to hear your story. You may say you are afraid of public speaking. I'm not going to minimize that; you probably are afraid. Fine. Research public speaking. Once you do it and do it well, it is a rush.

DREW

BEING A FATHER is the greatest responsibility a man can have. The only thing better than being a father is hearing a child refer to you as *Daddy*. The day in October of 1987, when Patrick was born, saw me cry . . . uncontrollably. I had heard that the tears of joys and tears of pain are comprised of different chemicals. That day in '87 confirmed it.

August 1989, my wife Pam used an over-the-counter pregnancy test. It was indicating that what we had been hoping and praying may come to pass. So, to remove all doubt, Pam made an appointment with her OBGYN. I came home from work that afternoon. Pam looked at me, smiled and said, *Hi Daddy*.

I said, *I knew it!*

I decided Patrick's name. This would be Pam's turn. If it was to be a girl, she would be *Megan Elizabeth*; if a boy, *Drew Christopher*. As with Patrick, she did not want to know if it was a boy or a girl until it was born. Unlike when Patrick was preparing for this world, this time I did want to know the gender. A few months after we learned Pam was pregnant, I accompanied her to the OBGYN for a normal check-up.

An ultrasound was performed. The technician knew Pam did not want to know the gender. She also knew I did want to know. The ultrasound displayed the baby's image on the screen. The technician looked at me and said, *See?* I acknowledged. It was a boy. Trust me.

One morning in May 1990 after many false alarms, Pam woke and told me that it was time. You need to know there were also false alarms with Patrick. It was early in the morning, and the baby was not due for a couple more days. Besides, I'm not a morning person. I find it difficult to function until that first cup of coffee. Out of absolute chivalry, I did get up. Was able to find the coffee pot, walk to the bathroom and splash water on my face. Pam was waiting patiently. Then as I was in the bedroom picking out clothes to wear, I heard Pam say, *Greg, I've gone to have a baby. I'll call you later.*

Oh, she's not kidding! So, I put my body in overdrive and took Pam to the hospital. Pam's parents would bring Patrick to the hospital to welcome his brother into the world. As with Patrick's delivery, this would be a C-section, which is good for the baby but can play havoc on the mother. On May 13 Drew Christopher Little arrived weighing 9.9 pounds with a full head of hair.

Our house had become a home with four people. I was working full-time and attending school full-time. Pam was working at a ceramic shop. Patrick was not yet 3-years old, and Drew, who had recently arrived in the world, had the makings of a future linebacker. Or, so it seemed.

He was born with no complications, but after a few weeks Drew was unable to keep food down. We took him to the pediatrician, who diagnosed Drew with pyloric stenosis, which means the muscles in the lower part of the stomach through which food and other stomach contents pass have become enlarged to the point where food is prevented from emptying out of the stomach.

Consequently, at 6-weeks old, Drew had his first operation. Because he had become dehydrated and his veins had constricted, it was difficult for medical personnel to find a vein for an IV. Hearing Drew cry as he was being stuck with needles, as we waited in the adjacent room, was a helpless feeling many parents have endured. Even so, knowing that did not lessen our anxiety. Finally, the nurse brought Drew back to us and said, *I'll try again tomorrow. I'm not going to hurt him anymore.*

We may think that medical personnel have tough skin, because they have to perform procedures that can result in patient pain. It's good to see when they show empathy for people under their care.

Things seemed to be better. After the surgery Drew was able to keep food on his stomach. I was working full-time and was able to concentrate on my doctoral study. At three-months into his life, I noticed what seemed to be a glaze on Drew's eyes. I did not mention this to Pam. This will sound crazy, but I thought that might be normal for infants . . . or maybe I was just scared it would be *something else*, which I was afraid to face.

My fears came true. We were visiting Pam's parents in early September, and my brother-in-law, Phil, was on the couch holding Drew. Phil looked in Drew's eyes and told Pam that something was wrong with Drew's eyes. We looked at Drew and realized Phil was correct. The following day, an appointment was made with an optometrist in Jackson, 87 miles away. We need to stop here and say that taking a 3-month-old baby for an eye exam is not a normal experience.

The optometrist looked at Drew's eyes through what I think was a slit lamp. Drew was crying. He was scared from all the change . . . and having his little eyes held open. After the optometrist examined Drew's eyes, he stepped out of the room and came back with his partner. His partner examined Drew's eyes, and the two talked with one another in medical jargon. Both had very stoic expressions. The tone of the voices was not reassuring. Pam said she would take Drew to the restroom and change him.

As Pam was leaving the room, the two physicians remained silent. After Pam had taken Drew out of the room, I said, *Alright gentleman, what's the verdict?*

They looked at one another, and the older one said, *This is serious.*

I sat down. It was then that I was informed my 3-month old son had cataracts. Pam returned to the room in a few minutes.

After explaining the conditions of Drew's eyes, we were given the options. Surgeries could be performed to remove

Drew's lenses, and he could wear contact lens, which we would have to put in and out every day. The other option was to do nothing, and he will go blind. We were told to go home, think about it and make a decision in a couple of weeks.

There was no need to go home and think about it. We wanted to give Drew a chance of sight. We chose the surgeries. They told us of two very prominent eye surgeons in Hattiesburg, Drs. David Richardson and Stoney Williamson.

An appointment was made for Drew to have one of his lenses removed. The other would be removed in the two-weeks following. Both would be outpatient surgery. Dr. Richardson performed the surgery with Dr. Williamson assisting.

After the surgery, Drew was brought to us in a private waiting area. A patch was covering his right-eye, which had the surgery. He was alert and not in any distress. In a few weeks, surgery on the left-eye was performed. This time when Drew was brought to us, the patch was off the right-eye and one was on the left-eye.

At five months old, Drew began wearing contacts. Obviously, the contacts he was to wear would not be permanent. There were two reasons for this. At five-months old, he would continue to grow, and the contacts would not. Also, any contacts he would wear would have to be a good estimate. It would not be possible for Drew to take an eye exam. At five months old he could not say, *I see the big E.*

Dr. Richardson had to make an estimate of needed strength of the lenses. He estimates were good. His vision was noticeably improved. We were told that he could probably never play tennis or golf but could play volleyball and basketball. That would be ok . . . as long as he had a quality of life. We had gone over a hurdle. Things would get better, or so we thought.

Pam had to put contacts in his eyes twice each day. Insurance at the time would not pay for the contacts. So with every contact was a cost of $100 that we certainly did not mind paying, as long as it allowed Drew to have sight. Yes, there were some horror stories. He lost one in the backyard the first time he wore it. That contact would never be seen again.

I don't know how Pam did it. With me working full-time and going to school full-time, she was working full-time at a crafts shop, raising two little boys, one of whose eyesight was totally dependent on her.

Drew was a pretty baby. He had long hair that curled in the back. He also had long eye-lashes. Often we would take him somewhere, and people who had not met Drew thought he was a girl. As the next few months passed, I saw Pam work tirelessly. She always wanted children, but we never thought a child of ours would be wearing contacts at five months.

By the time Drew was 11 months old, a film had developed over his eyes. This time we didn't wait. We made an appointment for Drew to be seen by Dr. Richardson. The film would have to be removed. As with the original cataract surgery, Dr. Richardson would remove one film, put a patch on that eye and perform the same procedure on the other eye a couple of weeks later. At 11 months of age Drew had undergone five operations - one on his stomach and four on his eyes. Surely life would begin to resemble normalcy.

Drew would sleep all night, every night. He did not seem to thrive as other babies. His face was getting very full. When we would take him to the nursery at church, other babies would run around, crawl around, laugh and play; however, Drew would just sit in a swinging chair and watch the other children play. Perhaps he was just going to be a little slow at starting to walk.

May 13, 1991 was his first birthday. We had a birthday party for him with a cake, gifts and a ton of cousins and relatives. Something was not quite right. Drew was very sluggish. His body seemed bloated like he had gained weight and he showed an apparent total lack of energy.

The following day, Pam and I took him to see his pediatrician in Hattiesburg. Dr. Merritt did a thorough exam, which included an x-ray. As Pam and I waited in the exam room, a nurse brought Drew to Pam. Dr. Merritt came in and reluctantly said, *Well, come in and hear the verdict.* An x-ray of Drew's chest was on the screen. Dr. Merritt pointed to the chest cavity, and said, *This is his heart,* then pointing to a smaller area he said, *This is where it's suppose to be.*

Dr. Merritt was explaining to us that Drew's heart, and we would soon learn his liver, were enlarged. He had caught a virus, Cocci-B, from the air or somewhere. The reason he looked so *puffy* was due to fluid retention, which was secondary to his enlarged heart.

Dr. Merritt informed us that the University Medical Center (UMC) in Jackson, which was 90 miles away, was waiting on us. We were to take Drew to the ICU. Dr. Merritt said, *Go home, put some clothes together and don't dillydally around. This is serious.* I knew it was. As Dr. Merritt was saying this, a tear was coming down his cheek.

Before we left his office, Dr. Merritt made an appointment for Drew to receive an injection at the Forrest General Hospital in Hattiesburg. We were to do this, go home, pack some clothes and rush to UMC. The injection at Forrest General Hospital was to make Drew void so he could lose all the fluid he had retained. Did it ever!

To be blunt, following the shot, Drew wet his diaper like I'd never seen. We rushed home, called Pam's mother, Sally, who would take care of Patrick while we were gone. We put some clothes together, put Drew in the car and with my emergency flashers on, we quickly began the 90 mile drive to Jackson.

About halfway there, I realized that I had left my clothes in a travel bag inside the door at our house. Stress will play havoc on one's organizational skills. Drew slept during most of the drive to UMC. By the time we arrived Drew was a new kid. All of the weight he lost from urinating had vividly made him much happier. He was showing more life, which was a shot of confidence for us.

Dr. Merritt was correct. The staff at UMC was expecting us. Drew was given a private room in ICU. Though his was a small room as hospital rooms go, his bed was big enough for a pro football player. There was one chair, which would become Pam's bed for the next three nights. The bathroom had a sink and a toilet. UMC is a very large but old hospital. The facilities are perhaps in some ways not ideal; however, due to the fact it is a medical center used to train medical students, the care is incredible.

At the end of the first day, I drove home to Hattiesburg and checked on Patrick, who was 20 miles away in Laurel. The next day I drove back to Jackson to be with Pam and Drew. This time I remembered to bring my clothes and stayed with our friends, Bobby and Susan Stephens.

On the third day at UMC a friend from our Sunday School Class, Mike Landrum, drove from Hattiesburg to UMC to visit with us and take me to lunch. Mike had played football for the Atlanta Falcons after playing at our alma mater, Southern MS. His act of kindness meant a great deal to me. It's comforting to see people regarding their size or persona, not being afraid to show love for a friend.

Drew's physician informed us that he would prescribe Lasix and Lanoxin to treat Drew's enlarged heart and enlarged liver. After four nights in the hospital, we were discharged to return home. Naturally, there were the post-discharge instructions, and they reminded us again of the seriousness of Drew's condition. He cannot be startled. His heart cannot withstand stress. He cannot get the flu . . . his heart would never be able to withstand it as well.

After hearing all of these precautions and instructions, coupled with Pam having to give Drew's medicine to him twice a day, as well as put his soft contacts in his eyes, an obvious decision would be made. Pam would have to quit her job at the ceramics shop.

While I was working full-time at a facility serving individuals with chemical dependency and going to school full-time, Pam was taking care of a very sick infant and trying to raise a 3-year old child. Her *job* was totally full-time.

Most of the evenings, when I came home from work/school; Drew would be sitting in a highchair facing the door. As I would come in the door I would often take him out of the highchair, hold him and talk with him for a while. However, there were also many nights I would come home, go in the door and Drew would look at me with an eager look in his face, while I just said, *Hi, Drewster!*

Then I went to my study and work on my dissertation. As I sat at the computer I can vividly remember thinking, *When I finish my doctorate, I'm going to spend more time with Drew.*

Being an infant with an enlarged heart is bad. We watched as Drew's energy was often drained. He slept all night every night. In the mornings I would wake-up before anyone else. I went to the kitchen, get a cup of coffee and go to the boys' room. Patrick, sleeping in a single bed, would sleep as long as he could. I went to Drew's bed and wait there till he woke.

He almost always slept with his butt in the air. Pam said he was *rooting*, whatever that means. I would stand by his bed and wait until he woke. This was a ritual. He would wake, pull himself up by the rails on his bed and we would just look at each other and smile.

Keep in mind that Pam had not gotten up yet; consequently, Drew's contact lenses were not in his eyes at this time in the morning. If I ever started to walk away from his crib to get another cup of coffee, Drew would cry. I only went two or three steps and always came back. We would get back to smiling at each other as if nothing had happened.

After a few minutes passed, I would extend my arms, and he would reach for me. I picked him up and carried him to the master bedroom as Pam was waking. Before she got out of bed, I would bring Drew to her, and as I handed him to her, she would softly say, *Hey, Drew.*

As stated earlier, being an infant with an enlarged heart is bad; however, being an infant with an enlarged liver is worse. That will cause pain, much pain. Unfortunately, Drew had both. There were times when he would cry and scream from the pain, and there was nothing we could do.

At times we would lie him on the floor, and he would inadvertently, jolt his head back and hit his head on a chair-leg or table-leg. This would scare and hurt him, which made the crying and screaming increase.

Looking back it's hard to fathom that I didn't notice the things he could hit his head on if his body jolted back. We would dig at any straws to find some position to make him as comfortable as possible.

His contact solution had to be mixed a certain way. Pam was teaching Drew at a year old how to do it. Often when he had the strength to walk, he would carry the Lasix in one hand and the Lanoxin in the other hand as he brought them to Pam. He knew that when she gave the two medicines to him, they would help him to feel better.

During the time that Drew was in this condition, his brother, Patrick was 3-years-old. They loved each other very much. The cardiologist in Jackson told us that Drew could never withstand stress and did not need to be startled. There were times when Patrick, by just being a kid, would by accident do something that might startle Drew. I would send Patrick to his room, which caused him to cry. As a result, Drew would cry.

Patrick was very patient with Drew. If Drew was upset, I just said, *Patrick, tend to Drew.*

Patrick would get a toy shaker and shake it in front of Drew's face to calm him. Not bad for a 3-year old kid, huh?

Sometimes we would say to Drew, *Where's Drew's ears?* He would point to his ears.

Where's Drew's nose? He would point to his nose?

Where's the puppy dog? He would point to Kodiak, our dog.

Where's Patrick? He would look at Patrick and smile.

We never asked him to point to his eyes . . . for obvious reasons. Pam was now a full-time stay-at-home mom. She was taking care of an infant, who wore contact lenses, which had to be taken in and out at least twice a day. She had to make sure that an infant, who was weak and often in pain, had his medicine on time every day. She was trying to provide as normal a life as possible to that infant's 3-year-old brother.

All of this while her husband, who was working full-time and going to school full-time, was able to provide minimal assistance. One thing that I will never forget is that Pam always had Drew glued to her side. She was always carrying him.

Patrick was a very significant part of our family during this time, but for six-months Drew was Pam's world. We had to do all we could to prevent him from being startled, having an illness of any kind and constantly know the whereabouts of his contact lenses.

Every parent thinks their child is pretty . . . and rightfully so. Having worked and visited several institutions serving individuals with developmental disabilities, I have seen many people with birth defects. All have beauty in various ways. Once you get to know someone with a challenge, be it physical or mental, after spending some time with them, you notice that person is more like you than not.

At any moment without warning Drew would start crying with a piercing scream . . . his liver was hurting. Pam could give the medicine to him but could not administer the doses to Drew too close together.

Sometimes we would hold him in an effort to ease his pain. When that didn't work, as mentioned earlier, we would put him down thinking he needed no constriction. That would make it worse by the fact that at a little more than a year-old, Drew was unable to talk and tell us what was hurting. This was the most hopelessness I had ever experienced. That would change.

Drew had an appointment to be seen by his cardiologist on November 26, 1991. The week earlier, Drew began to show signs of a cold . . . perhaps an upper respiratory infection. He was having congestion and was weak. Pam took him to our pediatrician. Bronchitis. Now our fears were silent panic. I did not want to scare Pam by making a big issue out of it, which is ridiculous. It was like Dr. Bob Rhodes once said, *If we are all in a room sitting around a table and there is an elephant standing on the table, and think that if I don't say anything maybe no one will notice.*

On Sunday, November 24, we drove 24 miles to visit Pam's family, watch pro football on TV and have Sunday dinner. Pam's father, Chuck, and brother, Phil, would be there. Both worked for EnviroSafe, a company that provides emergency response and regulatory compliance programs to large organizations.

It was rare for Chuck and Phil to be home, because they were assigned to work on offshore oil rigs; however, Chuck had a severe upper respiratory infection and was unable to leave the house, much less go out to sea.

I was driving the car with Drew in his car seat next to me, Pam and Patrick rode in the back seat. After I parked the car at Pam's parents' house, I took Drew out of the car seat, it was fall; consequently, the leaves had either fallen to the ground or had turned colors.

As I came to the side door, my mother-in-law Sally came to the door and took Drew from my arms. Patrick, who was now four-years one-month old, went to play with his cousins. Pam went to the kitchen to help her mother and take care of Drew. My brothers-in-law and I were in the den watching pro football on TV. The den is adjacent to the kitchen. The kitchen and dining room are separated by a bar.

At 4:00 that afternoon Pam was in the dining room holding Drew in her lap and trying to persuade him to eat a few peas. Sitting on a sofa in the den next to the door going to the kitchen, I heard something I never heard in my life but instantly knew what it was. Pam screamed, *My baby! My baby!*

That instant, I knew Drew was dead. She immediately ran into the den fell to her knees, holding Drew and screamed, *Something's wrong with this baby!*

Drew looked as if there were no bones in his body. The area between his nose and upper lip had already turned blue. I said, *We've got to do CPR.*

I have taken CPR many times and have even taught it, as well as performed it once on a seven-year old child. However, at this instant my mind went blank.

Immediately after Pam came into the den with Drew, Chuck, who was very sick but adrenaline had kicked-in, said, *Put him on the bar.*

Phil immediately came to the kitchen and began mouth-to-mouth, while Chuck would count aloud and give him verbal support. As Phil breathed into Drew's mouth and nose, his little chest would expand and then go down.

Meanwhile, I was dialing 911 for an ambulance. After explaining to the dispatch where we were located, I asked if she would stay on the phone until the ambulance arrived. She gracefully obliged. Phil's wife, Debra, and Pam's younger brother, Chris, went to the road so to wave the ambulance onto the driveway.

When the ambulance arrived, I was able to hang-up the phone with the dispatch. The two paramedics came in as Drew lay on the bar. We would later learn they had no idea the person they were about to treat was an infant. They had a suction that was placed over Drew's face and used to continue CPR. After a few moments and as it appeared Drew might be breathing, one of them picked Drew off the bar and headed for the door.

Pam got into the ambulance with Drew, and I followed in our car alone to the hospital. It was a 7-mile drive. The entire 7-miles, I prayed audibly, *Please don't let Drew die. Please don't let Drew die.*

We arrived at the hospital and Drew was rushed into the emergency room. Pam's family soon met Pam and me in the waiting room.

Shortly afterwards, a chaplain came into the waiting room and spoke with us. He told us that he had seen Drew in the ER and it was very serious. He asked if there was anything he could do. Pam asked him to say a prayer. He did, but some of the words in his prayer, though very realistic, were not very comforting, i.e., . . . *if there is any slim chance Drew might live . . . .*

How, we don't know, but Pam's friends began coming to the hospital to be with us. Pam noticed that hospital personnel were coming out of the ER with tears in their eyes. A nurse, who Pam had known since she was in high school but not seen in a very long time, came out of the ER. The nurse did not know who Drew's parents were. When Pam saw her come out of the ER, she called her friend's name and said, *That's my baby in there.*

The nurse, stunned by hearing this, looked at Pam and without saying a word, went back into the ER. Shortly afterwards, hospital staff moved the entire family and friends into a separate room. I knew this was not a good sign.

The physician, who was attending to Drew, came into the waiting room, closed the door and asked what meds Drew was taking. We told him, and he stated, *We're going to do all we can.*

As he turned to go out the door, I asked him, *Doctor, is he breathing on his own at all?*

He paused, shook his head, *No,* and walked out the door.

Someone came into the waiting room and said there was a phone call for me. Going down the hall a few feet into a side room a phone was off the hook. I lifted the receiver. It was our Sunday school teacher, who was also one of Drew's pediatricians, Dr. Ronnie Kent in Hattiesburg. He stated that *they would probably stabilize Drew and rush him to Jackson,* which was 95 miles away.

However, the happenings in the last hour told me otherwise. Dr. Kent wanted to close our phone call with a prayer. The instant Dr. Kent said, *Amen,* the door in the ER opened and the attended physician was going into the waiting room.

My brother-in-law was in the hall and said, *Greg!*

I hung-up the receiver and walked toward the waiting room. As I took the few steps, the loud crying coming from the other side told me the verdict. I opened the door, and the first thing to catch my eyes was my brother-in-law, Ronnie, crying. I then turned to the left and saw our friend, Tracie Smith, crying as she held onto Pam. In a low tone I said, *He's gone?*

Then I held Pam and Tracie.

While Dr. Kent was on the phone with me, the attending physician came into the waiting room, looked down and without saying a word, slowly shook his head. Pam said, *He's dead?! Drew's dead?!* He nodded and left the room.

We would later learn that Drew had been pronounced dead for several minutes before the physician came into the waiting room. After the physician realized Drew was not going to make it, he walked around the ER hitting tables with his fist saying, *Why?! Why?!*

Then came the very uneasy task of phoning my parents, who were in their 70's, and telling them that their youngest grandchild was dead. My in-laws were doing all they could to take off as much responsibility from Pam and me as possible.

Back at the same telephone where I was talking with Dr. Kent, my brother-in-law, Chris, was on the phone with my father trying to relieve me from the chore of telling my parents that their youngest grandchild was dead. Chris was nervous and stammering. As I walked by, he handed the receiver to me and said, *I can't do it.*

Putting the phone to my ear, I said, *Dad.*

He replied with a laugh in his voice, *Hey Greg boy!*

I then said, *Dad, Drew's gone to Heaven.*

His voice lowered as he said, *Well* as if not knowing what else to say. My Mother was down the hall from my Dad but could hear when he said, *Hey Greg boy!* After Dad and I had that brief exchange, she picked up the receiver in their bedroom and in an upbeat manner, said, *Hello.*

Without thinking or knowing what to do, I said, *Drew's dead, Mother.*

I never heard her make another sound during the rest of the phone call. What happened after that, I cannot recall exactly. My parents had to make their plans to come to our house.

Looking back, I wish I could have found a better way of breaking the news to my mother. It is too bad the words that come out of our mouths do not come with an eraser.

As everyone was still in the hallway trying to decide what to do, I grabbed Pam's hand and led her into a separate room in the hospital, where we could be alone. I looked her in the eyes and said, *We're going to make it. We're going to get through this. Let's say a prayer.*

We held hands bowed our heads and I prayed audibly to ask God to tell Drew that we are proud of him. A nurse came out of the room, where medical staff had been working on Drew.

She came to Pam and me and stated, *After we get him cleaned up, you can come in and say, 'Goodbye' to him.*

A few minutes passed and the door to the room, where Drew was, opened. The ER doctor was sitting in a chair by the bed. A couple of nurses were in the room as well. We walked into the room, saw his still body and I said, *Hey Drew.*

We walked over to him. Pam said, *I want to hold him.*

We picked him up, and Pam held him in her arms. He just looked as if he was asleep. After a few moments, she handed him to me. I help him and kissed his forehead. Everything *looked* normal . . . then as he was in my arms, Drew's lifeless left arm fell and was hanging down. That did not *look* normal.

We laid him down on the bed. Pam gently opened his eyes and took out his contacts and placed them on the sheet. That was something the medical staff in the room were not expecting to see. As we stood over him, I thought to myself, *I want to kiss his little feet.*

That may sound strange, but if you want one last chance to touch your child . . . thinking the medical personnel in the room may think that would be too strange, I thought, *I'll kiss his feet later.*

There was no *later.* The next time I saw Drew was when we was in a coffin.

We left the room, and it was time to go back to my in-laws' house. Now Pam and I had the task of telling Patrick, who was four-years one-month old, that his baby brother would not be coming home. While we were at the hospital, Patrick was staying with Dee Dee, our sister-in-law, and Ronnie's wife. Ronnie's house was two houses from Chuck & Sally's house.

Pam and I got out of the car at Chuck & Sally's house and walked to Ronnie & Dee Dee's house. Patrick was in the back room playing. Patrick walked with us to the backyard.

Pam got on her knees in front of Patrick and explained to him that little Drew's heart just could not work anymore and quit beating. Patrick listened intently, moving both hands together as many people do when they are nervous. He understood as much as he could. Pam then asked him if he would like to go to the funeral home the next day and see Drew. Patrick replied, *Will there be blood?*

We assured him there would be none. We also agreed that seeing Drew in the casket might be more trauma than Patrick could handle.

When I got back to Chuck & Sally's house, I telephoned work and explained to the switchboard operator what had happened. After making that call, I telephoned Chuck Prestwood, who lived in Jackson.

Chuck and I worked together with the MS Health Care Commission as inspectors of institutions serving individuals with developmental disabilities (ICF's/MR). We first met in 1978, when he came to Oxford to inspect the ICF/MR where I was employed. However, in this instance I was phoning Chuck, because he had started The Compassionate Friends (TCF) chapter in Mississippi. TCF is a consortium of support groups developed to assist bereaved parents survive the death of a child. Chuck and his wife, Marlise, had a daughter, Krissy, die of Meningitis in 1975. After telling Chuck that Drew had just died, he replied, *Oh my, gosh.*

He asked what I needed him to do. I asked him to phone my good friend, Bobby Stephens, who lived outside of Jackson. Bobby and I had been friends since the mid 70's, and he was the best man in my wedding. After making that phone call for me, Chuck and his wife immediately began the 90 mile drive to Chuck & Sally's house in Ellisville.

I needed clothes for the next couple of days. So, as everyone else went to my in-laws, my brother-in-law, Phil, drove my car with me in it to our house in Hattiesburg, 26 miles away. They knew that I would be in no condition to drive . . . and they were right. After gathering clothes for the visitation and funeral, Phil drove me back to Pam's parents' house in Ellisville.

As we sat in the den that Sunday evening, a couple of hours after Drew had been pronounced dead, people began coming to the house to bring casseroles and other food. Watching this, the thought came to my mind, *Why are they doing this? Do they think we want to eat at a time like this?*

Eating was the last thing on my mind. What I didn't know at the time, was all these people were doing what they were suppose to do. When one's child or grandchild dies, one does not feel like cooking. One must eat, and we did.

Later it was brought to my attention that after a child dies, the bereaved parents will at times find anger in anything in order to vent their disbelief. Finding anger in people bringing food for us was not thought to be rational - but neither is burying your child. Thankfully, I never expressed that anger.

Within two hours, Chuck and Marlise arrived at the house. Chuck had conducted many workshops on the grief process that occurs after the death of a child. It was good having someone there, who knew exactly what Pam and I had been through.

More people came. Our minister, Dr. Gary Berry, who would conduct Drew's funeral, came with Dr. Kent, who was speaking with me on the telephone, when the physician informed Pam that Drew was dead.

Most of my life I lived near a town where there were street lights and store lights. Those were areas where viewing a clear sky at night to see stars was very rare. Pam's childhood experience was much different. She was a country girl. Clear skies at night to see . . . and count . . . the stars were a norm.

After everyone had gone home that first night and Chuck & Marlise had begun their journey back to Jackson, Pam and I walked into the backyard of her parents' house. As I held Pam in my arms, I saw a falling star. *Pam, look a falling star!*

By the time she turned to see the star, it was gone. Pam then told me that earlier in the evening Chuck told her that he had met Patrick in the hallway, who said, *If you see a falling star, it's Drew.*

We thought that was really an ironic coincidence.

The next day, Monday, Pam and I traveled to the funeral home to make the arrangements. The gentleman from the funeral home sat with us at a table in what looked like a conference room. A box of tissue sat on the table. With little input from me, which was how I wanted it, Pam made virtually all the plans.

She asked if Drew could be buried on his side as if he was asleep. The gentleman said they would try, but it would depend on how much his limbs will bend. As he was explaining this to her, I said, *Have you seen Drew?*

He nodded his head, *Yes.*

I continued, *He's pretty isn't he?*

He said, *Yes*, as he reached for a tissue.

That afternoon, was the visitation at the funeral home. Pam and I along with her parents and my parents arrived first. Many times in my life, people used the phrase, *It made my knees buckle.*

We entered the foyer of the funeral home and were directed to go into the room were Drew was in his casket. Turning at the door and seeing Drew, our infant son, in a casket, my knees did buckle. It was as if they were mush. I had to catch myself before going down.

What really looked odd to me was how tall Drew looked. Then it occurred to me, virtually all his life he had been in pain or was too weak to stand-up straight.

The number of people, who had come to visit, was a tremendous shot in the arm for Pam and me. The most important thing we needed was the hugs. Chuck and Marlise Prestwood were there every day. While at the funeral home, I mentioned to Chuck that it was great having all these friends showing this much concern. Chuck replied, *It will last three weeks. After that, no one will mention Drew to you. They won't want to 'remind' you of him.*

Chuck knew what he was saying. He was off by two days. After three weeks and two days, the phone calls, visits people asking how we were doing, stopped.

That night we had the same pouring of love from our friends, as well as our peers in the health care field. Later when everyone had gone home, Pam and I were again in the backyard hugging one another in the same spot as the previous night. Pam said, *Greg, look a falling star!*

By the time I turned around, the star was gone. We found that a bit odd, but we each saw a falling star two separate nights in row. We briefly discussed what Patrick told Chuck the day earlier, *If you see a falling star, it's Drew.* What was even more unusual about that is that in his then brief four years on earth, neither of us remembered mentioning anything to him about a falling star.

The next day at the funeral the love and concern shown by our friends and family really made me step back and realize how much people really cared. I remember seeing my Uncle Kendrick, who is a veteran of World War II, cry when he saw Drew in a casket.

Many people in the state from the executive branch of the MS Dept. of Mental Health came to Drew's funeral. Among these were Dr. Randy Hendrix, Roger McMurtry, Ed LeGrand, Ed Butler and their wives. Several friends working in the field of developmental disabilities came to offer their condolences, included were Suzy Lassiter, Larry Sherman and so many others it would be impossible to recall. These individuals are mentioned, because that day is like a *dream* to me, making remembering names next to impossible.

The professors in my doctoral field, Drs. Willie Pierce and John Rachal came. My nephew, Fred, and his wife, Kelly, drove from Texas. All of those people, along with many more, being there meant a great deal to me.

At the funeral Dr. Gary Berry presided over the ceremony. A tear was coming down his check as he began by looking at Pam and me and saying, *I don't know what to say to you.*

Nonetheless, he did an incredible job.

At the gravesite droves of people were in line to hug Pam and me. Many of my co-workers were there. Most of it was a blur making it impossible to remember all who came. One of few exceptions was a young lady, who had been one of the patients attending my weekly groups on the psychiatric unit at the Pine Grove Recovery Center in Hattiesburg. She had bulimia. She also professed to be an atheist. After she was discharged from Pine Grove, she developed a friendship with Pam and me. She stood in the line waiting to give her condolences. When she got to me, she said, *Greg, I'm so sorry.*

Upon hearing my reply, *It's ok. I know where he is, and I'll see him again.*

She tilted her head and gave me a *Children of the Corn* look as if to say, *Huh?*

The other person, who I vividly remember was the last person in the line . . . and it was a very long line was Robert Locke. Robert had been my initial advisor when I transferred to USM in 1975 and begun working toward an undergraduate degree in therapeutic recreation.

In 1978 he became my supervisor, when I started employment on the MS Gulf Coast as the therapeutic recreation director at a facility serving individuals with developmental disabilities. More than that, Robert and his wife, Susan, had become my very good friends.

When the line came to the end, Robert was waiting to give me a huge hug. He may have said something. That is impossible for me to recall, and it's not important. The hug was.

A week later, someone at work told me the young lady, who had given the *children of the corn look* to me, had become a Christian. A few days later, I saw her in the mall in Hattiesburg. I had to know. How was I going to approach the once professed atheist? She hugged me and asked how I was doing. This would be my chance. Again, my words were, *It's ok. I know where he is, and I'll see him again.*

A smile immediately came across her face, the kind of smile that will give *crow's feet* to one's eyes. She nodded an affirmative, *Yes!*

A little more than four weeks after we buried Drew, a secretary from our church phoned asking if I would give a testimony about Drew the next Sunday night. The night before I was to speak, Pam and I were sitting on the edge of our bed. Patrick was playing under the sheets. You might as well know that Patrick was always playing when he was a kid. He went on one speed – overdrive. Pam got emotional as we were talking about Drew and began to cry. Patrick pulled the sheet down from over his head, and said, *Why are you crying, Momma?*

Pam replied, *It's ok, honey. We're just talking about little Drew.*

Patrick said, *Don't cry, Momma. If you see a falling star it's Drew.*

That was it. I had to know. I said, *Patrick who told you that? Who told you that if you see a falling star, it's Drew?*

His entire demeanor changed. His face became very stoic; some would call it a *poker face*, as he replied in a very serious tone, *God.*

WHAT TO DO WHEN YOU ARE HURTING

SHORTLY AFTER DREW died, one of Pam's friends was going through a very traumatic experience. She was in an unhealthy and abusive marriage. She had two beautiful girls. One was the age of Patrick, and one was two years older. This lady, Rhonda, was a registered nurse and had worked very hard to get through college, and her father offered no support, neither financially or emotionally.

In a tumultuous marriage, Rhonda had to take the girls and move away from her husband. She was distraught. It was as if she was a body of nerves on two legs. We moved Rhonda and the girls into out house with us. Pam was busy taking care of Patrick and Rhonda's girls. Rhonda was trying to work while not becoming a basket case. Both attempts failed.

At the time I was working in an in-patient recovery center, which served individuals with psychiatric issues, as well as individuals with chemical dependency. Though my time was spent almost exclusively on the chemical dependency unit, once a week I presented a session on stress management on the psychiatric unit. This allowed me to become familiar with medical staff on both units. One such professional was Dr. Diane Little, no relation to me. Dr. Little was a rather new psychiatrist who brought new down to earth ideas to the facility.

While at our house one Sunday, Rhonda had a mental breakdown. She was crying and shaking uncontrollably. She needed help . . . immediately. Phoning the psychiatric unit, I learned Dr. Little was not on call that day. I wanted her to treat Rhonda. So, the only other option was to phone Dr. Little at home. After this was accomplished, Dr. Little told me to take Rhonda to the psychiatric unit.

The admitting orders would be phoned-in before I got there. Staff at the facility was expecting Rhonda when we arrived. For the next several weeks, Rhonda stayed at the facility while Pam and I took care of the girls. It was non-stop work. Having two boys in our lives for 18 months, and then going to one boy, then going to a boy and two girls was an adjustment.

Girls are different from boys. I did not know that. Growing up with two brothers and then having two sons was the only world I knew. Don't get me wrong. I know boys and girls are different. My Momma never raised a dummy. To the extent the sexes are different at a very young age was something I was about to learn.

Pam had to give me a cram course in parenting a multi-children household. Thankfully, Pam is great working with children. That is what she always wanted to do. When possible, I would take all three kids to school. This impromptu parenting kept us busy . . . very busy.

By the time Rhonda got out of treatment, she was a new person. She was much calmer and again had a great relationship with her girls. In a few weeks, she and her girls were able to move into an apartment and start a new life. Shortly after she moved into the new apartment, Rhonda thanked us for helping her survive her situation so soon after burying Drew. My reply to her was, *No, thank . . . you. Being able to take care of you and the girls kept us from thinking constantly about Drew's death.*

What did we learn from being caretakers for a few weeks? When you are hurting, help someone else who is hurting. Being able to focus our attention on Rhonda and the girls, helped us not to focus so much on us. In my mind losing Drew was much more traumatic than what Rhonda had to face, but in her eyes, the issue she was living was more traumatic. It was impossible for her to feel our pain, but she did feel her pain.

THE PARKING LOT

WHEN PATRICK WAS 11 months old, he had to be placed in a hospital in Jackson due to dehydration. The physician ordered X-rays. Patrick was unable to keep food down and was misdiagnosed with gastro esophageal reflux. His inability to keep food down was all but constant. His food came up so much and so violently that we had to change the carpet in the living room and den.

When he was nine-months old, he weighed 19 lbs. When he was one-year old, he weighed 19 lbs. Yet, when Pam took him for a check-up, the nurses would say that he is *thriving*. Pam hardly thought 19 lbs at one-year old was *thriving*.

Shortly before his 5th birthday, Patrick was diagnosed with malrotation of his intestines by Dr. Merritt, our pediatrician in Hattiesburg. To put it in layman terms, Patrick's intestines, should have been in a straight line, however, his were twisted causing obstruction and death to that part of the gut. Dr. Merritt recommended we take him to Dr. Richard Miller in Jackson at the University Medical Center (UMC).

Dr. Miller is an excellent pediatric surgeon. An appointment was made for us to take Patrick to see Dr. Miller for an initial visit. We did not tell Patrick the reason for the visit. He had been through enough in his short life. Dr. Miller's rapport with children has no rival. He made all of us feel at ease. Patrick still did not know the reason we were there.

Oh, you may remember that Patrick had been misdiagnosed with gastro esophageal reflux. We later learned that the medical staff, which treated Patrick when he was eleven-months old, lost the X-rays. Apparently, the physician made an educated guess. Unfortunately, for Patrick it was the wrong guess.

The surgery performed by Dr. Miller was a complete success. Being treated at a teaching hospital was a plus. The constant care and number of interns and nurses on duty was a much needed comfort.

There was one thing that happened when we brought Patrick for his initial visit with Dr. Miller. We drove the 90 miles to UMC and parked in the back at the pediatric clinic, a place Patrick had never been. When we found an empty spot in the parking lot and turned off the ignition, Patrick screamed and tried to lock the doors, *No! No! This is where you brought Drew! This is where you brought Drew!*

He was right. It was the same place we brought Drew, when on his first birthday he spent four nights in ICU. It was the place we brought Drew, a place Patrick had never been.

I KNOW HOW YOU FEEL

BEFORE MEETING THE lady, who would become my wife, fate allowed me to become involved with The Compassionate Friends (TCF). Twice in the early 1980's for their annual convention, Chuck Prestwood asked me to supervise children's activities, which allowed their parents to attend the conference. Doing so and my many conversations with Chuck allowed me to learn a great deal, initially from an *outsider's* viewpoint about the death of a child.

Because of these encounters years ago, I knew that Pam and I needed to embrace TCF without hesitation. We desperately needed to hear someone say, *I know how you feel*, who had walked in the same path. After going back to work, a few days after Drew died; people would say to me, *I know how you feel. My grandmother died*, or *I know how you feel. My dog died.* It was like talking to people from outer space. It would be virtually impossible for them to know how we felt.

For a few years, we did embrace TCF. The first time we went to TCF was for the Christmas meeting a couple of weeks after losing Drew. Because it was Christmas, there was a buffet. Going through the buffet in front of Chuck and Marlise, we mentioned to them that we were really feeling pretty good. Everyone within hearing distance from us, turned and either said or agreed, *You're in shock*. They were right. They were very right. Since then, a great deal of information about the grief process has landed in my brain.

The first six months after becoming bereaved parents, Pam and I were numb. We felt practically nothing. One exception was when I came home from work each day. My entire body would ache. Grief is hard physical work. It will drain the body.

During the first six months, we had to work to love Patrick. That may sound strange, and it perhaps should. We love Patrick more than life itself, but being able to feel love for anyone during the first months was like searching in a large crowd for someone you have never seen. It's impossible to describe what it is like to have a child die, because I have nothing with which to compare it.

Perhaps the best it was described to me was during a TCF meeting. If you bury your parent, you lose your past. If you bury your spouse, you bury your present. If you bury you child, you lose your future.

One of the hardest things we had to do those first few weeks was returning the toys that we had gotten Drew for Christmas. The lady, who assisted me with the return, said, *Did he not like it?*

It is important to know that the initial shock is not always six months. It could be four or five or seven or more. Six months is just the norm. There are many things about grief that are generic; however, everyone grieves differently. There is no right or wrong way to grieve.

After the initial shock begins to wear off, it is not uncommon for a spouse to learn that he or she has changed, as well as his or her spouse. There is a belief that there is a much higher divorce rate with bereaved parents. While there is a high divorce rate, professionals have told me that it is really not higher than the normal population.

There is a difference. Intimacy. Our physical relationship had noticeably diminished. One night at our monthly TCF meeting, a gentleman, who had written a book on bereavement, was our guest speaker. After an excellent presentation, the ladies went to one room and the men to another so that we might have gender friendly discussions. This was something we had not done during previous meetings, and we were curious as to how it would develop. After the ladies left and closed the door, one of our male members began to moderate. All was silent. Finally, being the not so shy fellow, I said, *I have a question, 'Intimacy'?*

That one word created an automatic response from everyone . . . even the guest speaker. Every man in the room said, *That's over* or a very close proximity to those two words.

In a way it was assuring to know that I was not the Lone Ranger. Pam told me that she did not feel as if she had the right to feel good, if Drew could not feel good.

January 1992, two months after Drew died, was the last time Pam told me that she loved me. It had nothing to do with anyone's fault; though I do believe there were times when I was not very lovable. That will be explained later.

January 1994 saw me employed as a quality assurance coordinator at another center serving individuals with developmental disabilities. Pam was working as a teacher's assistant to supplement our income. One day in November of the next year I was having a telephone conversation with my friend, Bobby Stephens, in Jackson. At that time Bobby was director of Rehabilitation Services at a large state hospital located outside of Jackson, which treated individuals with mental illness.

I had learned there was a position open for a coordinator of Restorative Therapy. Restorative Therapy was an umbrella term for physical therapy, occupational therapy, kinesiotherapy, speech therapy, audiology and creative arts. It required me to supervise 18 staff members. Bobby described what the position would entail. I applied for the position, was interviewed by individuals working in each discipline and began the first of December 1995.

Two or three years later, Bobby accepted a position as director of another division, which meant we no longer worked together. The middle of 1999, I had a telephone contact from a director in yet another division at the hospital. He was offering a job to me in which I would not be required to supervise anyone. It would be a lateral move in salary but with much less stress. I took it and never looked back.

The position was patient advocate at one of the largest state funded psychiatric hospitals in the nation. It would enable me to see and meet with patients, as well as develop corrective action to take whenever a patient's rights had been violated. The new job would prove to be less stressful, as well as allow me to moonlight by conducting my workshops and seminars.

The change in employment to work at the state hospital was a significant increase in salary. It allowed Pam to submit her resignation and enroll as a full-time student working on a degree in special education. There was one drawback with this job. I would have to locate at or near the hospital. From our house to the hospital was 87 miles.

The first five years, I lived on the hospital grounds in staff housing. For this I was much appreciative. I would get-up early on Mondays, drive to work and be there by 8:00 AM. On Wednesdays after work I would drive home to be with Pam and Patrick. Early Thursdays I would get-up and drive the 87 miles back to the hospital to be there before 8:00 AM. Then, drive back home Friday after work. This routine became a weekly ritual for five years.

Patrick was eight-years old when this ritual began. I would come home on the weekends to see that he had changed. He began his high school years, and I was working a job that was providing for his and Pam's basic needs, but I was not there to help him at night with his homework and help him through the normal things boys go through in high school.

Trying to convince myself that my choice of employment was the best for my family, it made me realize that many professions required the primary provider to be away from home as much if not more than mine. Many times life does not turn out the way we plan. Dwelling on the *what-if* would do nothing but set me or anyone, who did that, up to lose.

Meanwhile, Pam and I were growing further apart. Though I phoned her every night I was away, our conversations normally focused on paying bills or Patrick's issues with school or him competing in baseball or basketball. We never said the

D word – divorce. Sometimes I would ask her if she ever thought about not being married.

In March of 2000 I had booked a speaking engagement at a conference in a northern state. We agreed that after I got back from the conference we would talk about ending the marriage. The weekend before I was to speak, I came home on Friday and went back to work on Monday as usual. That night, when speaking with Pam on the telephone, she seemed very quiet. After asking her what was wrong, she replied, *Greg, I'll go ahead and tell you. I met with an attorney today and applied for a divorce . . . I've already moved out.*

This was somewhat of shock; yet, it was also somewhat of a relief. Pam stated that when she told Patrick, he got a little upset but was then excited that he and I would spend more time together.

In September, six months later, the divorce was final. The divorce papers stated that I would have Patrick every other weekend; however, Pam and I agreed that because Patrick at the time would soon be in junior high school, we would let him stay with me when he wanted regardless the weekend.

Since we divorced in September 2000, Pam and I have a relationship as former spouses that many would pay to have. However, many divorced couples tell me they too became closer friends following their divorce.

Society's perception of *divorced* has changed drastically over the last few decades. Back in the 60's in my small hometown with a population of 13,000, when a couple got a divorce, the entire town knew about it.

Literally. Now, sadly it's almost commonplace. For years the possible reason of this change in perception of divorce puzzled me. Was it because we normally have both partners working? Did it have to do with the media? Speaking one day with a friend of mine, who was a college professor about 60 years old; I presented the question to him. *Why is the divorce rate so high these days compared to the 60's?*

His answer made good sense. He believed that many couples wanted to get a divorce just as much as they do now. It just was not socially accepted as much then as it is now.

Consequently, he continued, people stayed in a bad marriage for the fear of the stigma of getting a divorce. It made me think, *He might be on to something.*

Back in the 60's a divorce in a small town did carry a negative connotation. In case you are wondering, this man and his wife have been married for more than 40 years.

RELATIONSHIPS

RELATIONSHIPS ARE OFTEN difficult. They take work. Most of us have an idea of how we hope our lives will turn out. Those ideas often involve another person. We hear that a relationship or marriage is 50-50, give and take. Shortly before my marriage, someone told me that the 50-50 theory is wrong. He stated that marriage is 100%. You have to be able to give up the last soft drink in the refrigerator. The taking part occurs when the other person gives to you.

When Pam and I were engaged, we were 24 and 30 years old respectively. Living alone for ten years, I was accustomed to having my own way. Pam lived in a household filled with people. This household was in the country outside of Soso, MS. Yes we are talking small. We are talking about a town with one possibly two police cars. Get the picture?

When we got married, she moved from a very small community in the country to the state capitol . . . literally near the actual state capitol. My job at the time required I travel throughout the state inspecting hospitals and nursing homes. Consequently, Pam was often alone, something she was not accustomed to.

After living in an apartment for nine years, I was now a married man. So, Pam and I decided to purchase our first house. We signed the papers in November 1985 and would take residence in the home the end of the next month.

Pam and our realtor, Susan Pinkston, found the house. Because it was in November, by the time I got off from work at 5:00 p.m., the sun was almost down. So, I saw the house for the first time at night. A few hours later, we paid the earnest money and signed the papers. By the time I saw it in the daylight, we were the new owners. I know. I know. The bank was the real owner, but we were the coming attraction.

Pam gave and adapted a great deal to my lifestyle. Joining the large Fitness Center I belonged and having to develop new friendships would be new things for Pam to face. It did not take a Rhode's Scholar to see that being alone sometimes at night was wearing on her. Perhaps getting a pet would help. Our friends, Bobby & Susan, had a cat. Opel.

Actually, they had about six cats, but at the time one was named *Opel*. Opel had a litter of kittens, and one of the kittens had kittens. We were given the opportunity to choose one of those kittens. It might be good to confess that at the time I hated cats. Very much liked dogs - but not cats. When we approached the kittens, one, a male, came right to us. This would be the one. Because his grandmother was named Opel, his name would be *Opie*. He was six-weeks old, tan & white and covered in fleas. Now can you see why I hated cats?

We immediately took him to a veterinarian. Opie weighed one-pound. That was before the vet took the fleas off. Afterwards, we took him home. My plans were for Opie to stay in a box outside on the back porch. We got home, gave the varmint cat food and placed him in his box. Pam's household companion, when I was away had set up residence, but he was not finished.

As I sat in my easy chair watching the old *Andy Griffith Show*, Opie (not to be confused with Ron Howard), was on the screen door on the back porch crying. He cried and cried . . . and cried.

I agreed to make a deal with him. He can come inside, but when he gets calm, he goes back outside. Picking him up and going back to my easy chair, I placed him on my chest. There, he began to knead me with his little paws. He began to make sounds that resembled a little engine running. It was apparent he was calm. It was also apparent he was glad he was on my chest and with me in my chair. He never made it back outside that evening. That night, Opie slept between Pam and me in our bed.

For the next three years, Opie did his job, which was to be company for Pam. He also became a member of our family. He could have easily been on *Most Incredible Videos*. Pam would give him a bath with the water hose in the backyard. She would hold him still with one hand and wash him with the other hand. He did not fight her. He followed me everywhere. We had a very close relationship. On a rare occasion, I would take a bath. Oh, that did not sound right. Let me rephrase that. Ordinarily, I shower. Sometimes I bathe in a bathtub. Sometimes when I bathed in a bathtub, Opie would sit in the tub with me and would not leave until the water reached his trunk.

I know what you are thinking – *here is some nut, who bathes with a cat.*

Whenever it was getting a little late in the afternoon, I would step on the back porch and yell, *Opie!* Hearing that one call, Opie would jump over the fence and come home.

There was an old stray cat with dark gray hair, which would on occasion come into our backyard. This was a wild cat with apparently no desire to be domesticated. One day this cat had cornered Opie in the backyard. Seeing this, my need to protect Opie went into high gear. Running out the back yard and with a very loud voice, I yelled, *Get out of here cat!*

That cat immediately leaped over the fence. Meanwhile, Opie stood still and was obviously relieved. Opie went into the house in my arms. When he heard and saw his owner running out of the house in anger, he knew that anger was not directed toward him.

One day when coming home from work, there was a note sitting on a bush outside the house. It was from Pam. Opie was injured, and Pam had taken him to an emergency animal clinic. He had been hit by an automobile, and his spine was broken.

Immediately phoning the animal clinic, I was given the news from the veterinarian. The vet could perform surgery, but the chances Opie would regain total movement were slim. We decided to have him put to sleep. Two days later, standing in our carport, Pam held me in her arms as I cried like a baby.

There is something about pets. They give unconditional love. Never noticing or caring about our flaws, pets love us in spite of ourselves. Perhaps we humans should take some lessons from our pets.

Like most males and many women for that matter, sports to various degrees have always been a part of my life. Understand, by saying *always a part of my life*, that is not meant to imply that I have excelled in anything. Nevertheless, to participate in organized or sandlot baseball, basketball, football was something that most kids did when I was growing-up.

Playing YMCA and Boys' Club baseball and playing intra-mural football in college like many young men, offered me the rather manly feel of occasional doing something to help my team win. I would add that I was on my high school baseball team -- but could not in good conscious say *playing high school baseball*, because there was not enough action off the bench to justify saying same. When we got married, I told Pam that I was a *world class athlete (WCA)*. She went along with it and even made a coffee cup in her ceramic class with *WCA* on the side.

After Patrick came along, he was involved in T-ball, Little League Baseball, Little League Football and Basketball. He became an excellent musician, primarily with the guitar. We were constantly going to college sporting events, sometimes professional baseball games, as well as concerts and Patrick's musical performances.

We learned that a family that laughs and plays together stays together. Sometimes things happen that causes the laughter to stop. After a few years, Pam and I realized that the feelings we once had for one another were in the past.

After our divorce was final in September 2000, an unfamiliar task was ahead of me. Dating. Not to say that I had never dated, but it had been 17 years since dating anyone other than my wife. It can be a real challenge to test the water after being with one person for a long period of time.

I have been given the opportunity to meet some very charming ladies, as well as a few that need to stay out of my playground. That is not to imply that they were wrong and I was right; though at the time in my emotional state, I may have thought they were wrong. It took me sometime to come to the realization of what you read earlier in the section regarding TBI, we did not come off a conveyor belt.

Regardless of the similarities some of us may share, we are all unique. You may not be able to comprehend why a certain person does not feel a certain way toward you. It could be that the feeling a person displays is all her or she is capable of. Our feelings are a result of our thinking, and it is virtually impossible to make someone think a certain way. We must learn to be accountable for our own experiences. You are who you are and where you are because of your input.

You are probably sitting as you read this book in a building . . . probably your home or perhaps a bookstore. Regardless of where you are, it is all related to the decisions you have made in your life. Those decisions may include the person you selected to spend the rest of your life with, the profession you chose, a place you were made to go due to your job . . . you were probably the one who completed the application for the job.

What is my point? Your decisions determine where you make your money, what company or group employees you, where you live, if you live with someone or alone. Once you accept that you must be accountable for your own experience, you begin to have power.

Power is a stark contrast from control. Power is about you. It is how you relate to yourself. You want to win. . . but you want others to win as well. This can be done.

Before thinking this is strange, allow me to tell you how to get anything you want in life. All you have to do is help other people get what they want in life. You do this, and people will give you power.

Another way power is different from control, because in control someone else is to be subservient . . . less than. You will usually get much more from people if you empower them rather than control them. This is not to say that some people don't need directions. The nature of many jobs will require that, but when possible if there is a problem let them be part of the solution . . . and of course thank them for their efforts.

Many people have been involved with someone on an emotional level, which later becomes a very negative experience. This person could have been a spouse, boyfriend or girlfriend. When the relationship dissolves, it is often difficult to comprehend how the relationship may have ended or why people behave in a certain manner.

It is important to know that most people we meet are battling some kind of a challenge. It could be low self-esteem, shattered ego, poor self-worth or a loss of trust.

You may believe someone you are involved demonstrates a narcissistic personality disorder. Should you hate someone, who has mistreated you? No. If you do, you lose. That is not to say that they win. That does not matter. They probably do not care either way. The point is — you lose.

Just stay away from them. Most of us, and I am including myself, have done things during our lifetime that others may consider narcissistic behavior. It is very important after you have stayed away from someone like this long enough, to forgive them. After you forgive them, you run out of excuses.

It may seem odd that I would state, . . . *after you have stayed away from them long enough, forgive them.*

If you can forgive them from the outset, that's wonderful; however, in all likelihood, that is not the norm. An experience like this will teach you to be careful who you invite to sit on the front row in our life. Some should sit in the back rows or in the balcony of your life. We need to love some people from a distance. Some have a history that allows us to know they do not deserve to be on the front row of our lives. Some we can love enough to be a few rows from us, some several rows from us and some from the balcony.

You will note that I stated, *Love enough to be a few rows from us.*

Depending on your situation, you may replace the word, *love*, with *like*, *view* or *tolerate*. Regardless, be very careful, of who you place in your front row.

My Dad said to me more than once that I can count my true friends, who will always support me, on one hand. There are many times that I have realized he was right. It is important to remember that everyone has flaws. It's not what we do with them that are important. It's what we do in spite of them.

During one of my presentations, a man asked why we would want to have someone, who brings total negativity, to even be in our life. Quite often we have no choice. They are just there.

Think of it like this. Be very careful who you invite to be on the front row of your life. Some we can keep in the foyer and some the parking lot. You may even know some who are best placed and left in the janitor's closet.

If you ask thirty people for their definition of love, you would probably hear thirty different definitions. After researching the views of many people and organizations, I will offer my definition of love.

As all definitions of love, it is imperfect. You can take from it what you like. Love is not a feeling one gets when they find someone attractive and hormones begin to fly, his or her heart pounds as if sending a message. Love is a choice. It is not just something you decide to do. It is both something you decide to do and the results of the decision.

Many people state that they quit loving someone, because the spark was no longer there. In reality they no longer feel in love because they quit fanning the flame. Marriage and love is work. If you think you will just float around with your partner in bliss for the remainder of your time on earth, I beg to differ.

There are some cultures where the parents of a newborn will make an arrangement with the parents of another newborn that their babies will marry when they become adults. These planned marriages have a lower divorce rate than marriages in America.

Why is the divorce rate as high as it is in America? Could it be expectations? We have an idea of our ideal mate or ideal marriage, and something happens to alter those ideas. This can be a change in health, the death of a child or change in our financial situation.

It may seem strange to some. The primary cause of divorce or a termination of a relationship in America does not involve intimacy or the lack of. It is money or the lack of.

It has been my privilege most of my life to surround myself with friends, who lift me emotionally rather than put me down. After a relationship I was involved had ended, a mutual friend introduced me to her neighbor, Shelia. I was facing the dilemma of being alone, and Shelia was recently widowed when her 49 year-old husband died in his sleep of an ulcer. He had not previously shown any signs of having an ulcer; consequently, this was a total shock.

A young vivacious man dying in the middle of the night from an ulcer, which no one knew he had, made her feel as if she was living a dream. Shelia had to dress him at two in the morning as neighbors, who she had just phoned, prepared to take him in their automobile to the hospital.

Shelia and her husband lived in the country; consequently, their neighbors' automobile would be quicker transport to the hospital than an ambulance. Yet, the entire time she was dressing her husband, she knew he was already dead.

Shelia and I became friends. You have some friends, whom you love. Shelia was one of those. She found no flaws in me. Unconditional love was a refreshing experience. It was a friendship love, but it was still a love. Though my flaws were apparent, she chose to accept me as I am.

A similar friend is Charlotte Newman, on the MS Gulf Coast. Over the past several years, Charlotte has become the type of friend that if either one of us needs someone to listen at 2:00 in the morning, just make the call.

Charlotte has faced her own challenges, such as working full-time when obtaining a graduate degree, surviving property damage and emotional trauma of Hurricane Katrina, just to name a few. Though she has known me for years, she has yet to find a flaw in me . . . not even one. Perhaps I should rephrase that. She like Shelia has yet to remind me of any of my flaws.

We often tell each other that we love one another. Though it is perhaps primarily a friendship love, it is love. She has chosen to love me. That is mutual.

Dr. Isidor Muniz became a close friend with my then-wife Pam, Patrick and me when Isidor and I went through our doctoral study together. *Izzy*, as he is known to his friends, lives in South Carolina. While living in Hattiesburg working on his doctorate, he lived in a small trailer with another friend, Dale Henry. You will read more about Dale in upcoming pages.

Izzy skipped one year in school and could have skipped two years. He is a very well read gentleman, which complements his vocation. He is a librarian . . . for grades K-12. He marched right after me during our commencement exercises in December 1992. Until 2006 he was librarian with a PhD for grades K-6 in a small town in South Carolina.

Though he lives several hundreds miles away, he manages to come to my residence, whenever it might be, and visit with me every year. He also goes to Hattiesburg every year to visit our major professor at USM, Dr. Willie Pierce and his wife, Carol.

Isidor always brings gifts. He never complains and accepts me regardless of my mood. In the twenty years I have known Isidor, it is impossible for me to recall a time when Izzy has complained. He always accepts people where they are in life . . . unconditionally. When life throws curves at me, it is good to have a friend that will lend a sensible, not patronizing, ear.

Those are only a few of the friends, who offer their friendship regardless my shortcomings. Mentioning all would be futile, and may result in some being omitted. Some people mentioned earlier, such as Bobby, Art and Robert would be included in that group.

I would have to include Avery Slay, though he may not have been mentioned earlier, I would be amiss not to mention Avery . . . even if he is a New York Yankee fan. I'm just kidding. The Yankees have fielded some great teams over the years.

STRESS

VARIOUS TYPES OF adversity have been mentioned several times in this reading. It would go without saying, though we will say it, that adversity is essentially always coupled with stress. Before we give stress a bad rap, it might be good to clarify some beliefs about stress.

The first is — not all stress is bad. Stress is good. In fact some stress can give us the energy to get a job done. Athletes are many times enabled by stress to perform at their peak. Stress or fear has given people strength to accomplish tasks they would not have been able to accomplish under normal circumstances. Coaches use the stress athletes endure before a big game to get his or her athletes prepared to play at their optimum level.

So, some stress is good . . . for a while. However, if we get too much stress our bodies will talk to us. The psychological effects of stress are fatigue, fear, anxiety, insomnia, reduced concentration, aggravation of psychiatric symptoms, worrying, inability to think clearly and lowered self-concept. It can also make the heart pound faster, cause people to breakout in hives, make hair fall out, cause ulcers, high blood pressure and eventually, death.

A good friend of mine was in the Marine Corps in the late 1960's in Viet Nam. One day his patrol was ambushed. He was the only one to survive. As he was lying on his back, he had his rifle in one hand across his chest and his bayonet lying by his side in the other hand.

He could see through his very slightly opened eyes, three Viet Cong coming to each fallen comrade and stabbing each Marine to make sure they were dead. As they were doing this, they were slowly making their way toward my friend. When they were about ten yards away and with my friend, who was unsure of his next move, to his total surprise Marines hidden in the jungle shot over him killing the three Viet Cong. After hearing him recollect his story, I said, *I would have defecated in my pants.*

He slowly turned to me and said, *I did defecate in my pants, Greg.*

Actually, this may not have been the exact word used.

In 1975 Robert Ader and Nicholas Cohen at the University of Rochester coined the term *psychoneuroimmunology*. Ader, Cohen and David Felton went on to write the groundbreaking two-volume book, Psychoneuroimmunology in 1981, which laid out the underlying premise that the brain and immune system represent a single, integrated system of defense.

In essence your brain cannot distinguish the difference between the threat to your ego and a threat to your life. It responds the same way. Most of us know someone, whose ego was threatened to the extent they became physically ill.

You may have heard of someone, who went through a stressful situation and shortly afterwards, died. In the summer of 1976, I worked at the VA in Biloxi-Gulfport, Mississippi. It was my internship and part of the requirements for an undergraduate degree in therapeutic recreation.

On the last day of my internship there was a fire at the nursing home of the Biloxi VA. All patients were evacuated safely and the fire finally extinguished. After this was accomplished, the director of the VA, Mr. Sheppard, went to his office, sat down at his desk and died. You probably have similar stories you could recall, as do I.

Let's talk about facts. Stress is the number one health problem in the world today. Each year in America, 75 to 90 billion dollars are lost due to stress related disorders. Ten percent of men currently 45 years old will not live to be 55 years old. The American Heart Association estimates that heart disease accounts for 52 million lost work days annually. One of four males will have a heart attack before retirement.

There is a 17 billion dollar decrease in productivity due to stress related mental disorders. Those disorders also result in 37 million work days lost each year. Americans consume 20 thousand tons of aspirin each year. Now we are taking about excess stomach acid!

Pain is the way the body talks to us. If you place your hand on a hot item, such as an iron, your hand immediately sends a signal to your brain to move your hand. If we eat too much, we feel full and stop eating. Likewise, an overload of stress is the way the body talks to us.

Unfortunately, too many times people experience the signals of too much stress, i.e., racing heart beat, sweaty palms and dry mouth, and say to themselves or someone else, *It's just stress.*

If it makes your heart race, lose sleep, headaches, *just* is not the word one should use to describe stress. The greatest stressor we have in life is change. We have more labor saving devices today than ever before but less time. We have cell phones, microwaves, internet and remote controls.

We no longer watch TV. We glaze. All these are labor saving devices; yet we are in a hurry more today than every before.

Change occurs so fast that it takes the human mind longer to process change than for change to occur. That is this maladaptive stress caused by change. Gradual stress is like a frog in hot water. If you put a frog in a pot of water on a stove and gradually turn up the heat, the frog will stay in the pot trying to adjust to the heat until it dies.

We are much like that. People will often stay in a stressful situation and not do something constructive about their situation until they experience a severe medical crisis.

According to the Journal of the American Medical Association (JAMA), our thoughts, without medical reservations, tend to keep us healthy or make us ill. Positive thinking does not always work; however, negative thinking works 100% of the time.

The great majority of self talk, 80% is negative talk. It is doubtful that you go home from work or school each day and say to yourself, *Wow! I was so good today. I really looked good today.* If you do, you have my congratulations. You probably will go home and say, *I cannot believe I said that. Oh, I wish I had said that in a different manner. Oh, I wonder what everyone is thinking about me.*

If it will make you feel better, I will let you in on a secret, those people who are the focus of your worries, are not thinking about you. They are too busy worrying what you are thinking of them.

JAMA has also found that happy people tend to be healthier, not just healthier people tend to be happy. What makes us feel good? Our thoughts make us feel good, and only we can control our thoughts. Granted, that is often easier said than done, but if you think good thoughts, you feel good. If you think bad thoughts, you feel bad.

No one can *make* you feel anything. The same thing can happen to five people, but all can have a different response.

We cannot see our stress and often cannot see our stressor. Because we want control, we look for someone to blame. Often that person, our victim, is someone we consider *less than us.* It can be a co-worker, a spouse, our child, virtually anyone. That is how most of us gain control, and it only leads to more stress. The minute our stress is someone else's fault, we are digging an emotional hole. Is that person going to change? Almost never.

That was a great deal of information about stress, but what is my point? I am glad you asked. Humor was my way to overcome much of my adversity.

Humor helps us getting off of blame as a mechanism for control. Humor is a way we gain control. There are two ways to bond with someone. Go through a hard time with them or laugh with them. I prefer to laugh with them.

When we laugh, our brain releases endorphins that act like morphine and numbs pain. How hard is it to release those endorphins? Right now, take a deep breath. Breathe in slowly through your nose and exhale through your mouth. One more time . . . in through your nose . . . and out through your mouth. Did you do it? How do you feel? Better, huh?

You might be thinking there are some things in your life that are not very humorous. I agree. There are some things that carry no humor; however, you can still get with someone, who can make you laugh. When you laugh, you purge your stress. When was laughter first used as a therapeutic tool? More than 2000 years ago. Proverbs 17:22, *A merry heart doeth good like a medicine, but a broken spirit drieth the bone.*

Until your adversity or challenge is overcome, stress will be your companion. The greatest stress we face in life is change. We plan for our lives, our bodies, our marriages and our careers, to be a certain way. That plan is usually for all of those things in our life to be successful.

Then life comes along and presents us with circumstances we do not expect. That causes change, our greatest stressor. Many times it is circumstances over which we have no control. Stress can alter our bodies. Our immune system breaks down making us easier to become ill.

The mind is an incredible tool. Our thoughts can keep us healthy or make us sick. How we look at things can very much play a key role in how negative things affect us.

Many years ago, I was having problems with anxiety. I was seeing a counselor once a week for this issue. Each week, he would tell me that I was the healthiest person he saw all week. It did not help me to know all of his other clients were in worse conditions than I. This is going to sound lame, but it was an eye opening experience for me. One day during our session, we were explaining my issues, and he wrote on his whiteboard, *So what?*

After seeing those words, it was like a bolt of lightning – what is the worse thing that can happen? In all likelihood nothing was going to happen that was really bad, and that proved to be the case. Things are going to happen to us everyday. Some things we just need to leave alone.

We worry about what others are thinking about us. Again, read my lips – they are not thinking about you. We are thinking about ourselves . . . and often we are worrying what you are going to think about us.

FROM GREATEST FEAR TO ULTIMATE CONFIDENCE BUILDER

YOUR MOUTH IS dry. Your knees are shaking. With white knuckles you hold onto the podium. That sucker might fly away, which leaves you essentially naked in front of all those people whose entire thoughts are on you. You open your mouth and to your chagrin, you have become a soprano! You are thinking, *Somewhere there is some lucky sap getting a root canal. He does not know how fortunate he is.*

Your fear of having to say the words on the page in front of you leave you with only one choice – say them faster. At least then this terrible experience will be over and you can sit down in shame.

It was my displeasure on July 5, 1979 to experience a root canal. It was abscessed. The anesthesia did not touch it. Even if my abilities to overcome my speech impediment had not been realized, I still would prefer public speaking to a root-canal. You will have to let me get back with you at a later date regarding the death issue.

Sounds like a tale of the extreme? To some it may. To others, such as me in my high school years, it is very real. Several studies have shown speaking in public to be the greatest fear faced by humans. This fear ranks higher than the fear death, heights, illness, you name it.

Why do we have such a fear? Could it be the fear of failure? Perhaps it is because we are wondering how other people are sizing us up. We are wondering what they are thinking about us. That fear is very real. Our bodies talk to us. Our palms become clammy. Our stomachs become tight. Our hearts are racing. In a sense we are our experiencing our own death.

Earlier you read that the human brain is often not able to distinguish the difference between the fear of failure and the fear of death. Alas, there is hope. Even though I regret to deflate your ego, I am obligated to assure you that the people in the audience are not thinking of you. They are thinking of themselves, which is the focus of everyone's thoughts most of the time – themselves. Or, they are wondering what the other fellow is thinking about them.

You might be able to relate to this fear. Having to stand in front of people staring at you in anticipation of what will come from your mouth that might enrich their lives can be a powerful experience. However, if the way you deliver your message is not conveyed in a certain way, you will be a failure. People will consider you a loser. They will go home and tell their spouses and children of how you ruined their day . . . or perhaps their week.

Worse, they may laugh while you are speaking or worse than that, throw rotten tomatoes at you. Not! None of this ever happens.

Kinda hard to believe, huh? Right now think about the best speech you have ever heard. That was probably not too difficult. Now, think about the worse speech you ever heard. Still thinking? If your speech is not hitting on all cylinders, people usually tune you out and think about their grocery list or the pretty lady on the other side of the room.

This writing is not to teach you to accept less than you want from yourself. Let's look at how you can do something others only wish they could accomplish.

If you are able to speak in public, you are able do something that most people avoid whenever possible. The ability to speak in front of a group will open more doors than most can imagine.

To command an audience, to hear the applause, for them to come to you at the end and tell you how much you meant to them, to know you left them feeling better about themselves and to hear them ask for an autograph. Humbly you gladly give them your signature after writing a few words of encouragement, while your ego is screaming, *Yes!*

All these things are the ingredients known as *speakers' high*, not to be confused with runners' high, but just as pleasurable.

The speaker Dottie Walters said that a speaker needs to think of his speech as food for the audience. A speaker must fill people up! People come to your presentation hungry for knowledge, hunger for a solution or a reason why. According to Dottie our job is to fill them up so when they go into the world they can solve their problems.

When preparing for a program, a speaker should go to the physical setting prior to his presentation. Perhaps you may need to adapt your speaking style in order to get mentally ready for the situation. Go to a few audience members prior to the presentation. Shake a few hands and introduce yourself. Ask each what they would like to learn before they leave the room.

By doing this you are developing a needs assessment and, more importantly, meeting a few friendly faces. Too, this demonstrates that you are audience driven.

It is good practice to meet someone, have them tell you their needs or desire for the seminar, and come back later to tell them that you have been thinking about their concern. You can also call the names of these individuals during your presentation.

Everyone has a need for recognition. By doing so, you have created a bond with that person.

When planning the wordage for your presentation, remember the old cliché, *Your job is to express not to impress.*

The average adult in America has slightly more than a high school education. Four out of ten adults have not graduated high school. Nearly three million Americans cannot read or write any language.

When you step up to the podium, stage or whatever your starting post, do it with confidence. Think of your audience as friends. Shake hands with a few at their seats before you have been introduced. The first words – or movements – should be to get your audience's attention. Jokes. If you cannot find a joke that applies to the audience or your topic, don't use it. Whenever possible, give personal experiences. They add feeling to a speech.

When I began speaking on a national level in 1989, the financial reward and providing for my family were two of the aspects that made it enticing. However, the primary reason my seminars were offered to the public was for the satisfaction of doing something that all my life had produced a fear worse than a nightmare. That may seem like a cliché, but it is the truth.

When speaking to a group that is quiet, still and hanging on to your every word as you give well-timed pauses is a rush. Having the audience roar with a deep belly laugh after they participate in a hands-on activity or give a standing ovation when you finish your presentation, will let you know . . . *You did it!*

What have I learned about public speaking? After you begin to do it, you will want to do everything possible to hone your skill. You will find in my bookshelf many books regarding public speaking. From the things you should and should not do to various means to overcome any fear you may have of standing in front of a group.

All through my formative years, through grade school and high school, I thought my speech impediment was a *no hope* issue. Since then, I have been given three ways to control my speech. That felt rather good to say . . . to control my speech.

All my life my speech impediment controlled me. In the upcoming years, I would learn either from speech therapists or individuals, who stuttered, three ways to control my speech. All three work.

The secret to all three is – I am the one who has to work them. So many people go to a speech therapist looking for a fix. They are expecting the therapist to do something to them that will make their speech roll off their tongues in a clear distinct manner. That is not going to happen. All the therapist can do is present the tools the client needs. It is up to the client to use them. Overcoming a speech impediment or any adversity takes work.

It is not easy. The only place you will find *success* before *work* is in the dictionary.

One such tool was given to me by a gentleman previously mentioned, Dr. Bob Rhodes. Due to my fast rate of speech, Dr. Rhodes taught me to pause. By pausing, the rate of my speech was and is greatly reduced. It is amazing . . . by just pausing . . . after saying . . . a few words . . . my speech is clearer . . . and the listener can follow . . . much easier . . . don't you agree?

You may think that it would be nice to be able to speak to a large group of people. You may also be thinking of why it would not be so nice *for you* to speak to a large group of people. You may think that you sound strange when attempting to speak in public. Then change your voice. Make it deeper. Not a great deal deeper, just enough for you to notice it.

Whatever you feel is preventing you from speaking in public, change it. It is very few public speakers who have not changed something about themselves to make their delivery clearer to the audience. Many speakers use a slightly deeper voice and utilize this new voice when speaking even to family members. Doing so over time will make the deeper fuller voice become natural.

If you think you talk too fast, slow down. Better yet, do something that will make you slowdown. Pausing, emphasizing the last sound of each word, use your fuller voice will all make at a slower rate. It may sound abnormal to you at first, but it will sound much more pleasant to the listener.

Remember this – there is no fix for it. Only you can make the change. You are only limited by your ability to adapt. Do not limit your ability to adapt. That philosophy has proven true to me in many situations. Many times people have over-come seemingly defeating situations by learning to adapt . . . modify.

What if you are speaking to an audience and someone asks a question to which you do not know the answer? Oh, and that will happen. Well, the last thing you want to say is, *I don't know*. My response is usually, *That is a very good question. Tell me, has anyone in the audience ever had this experience? If so, what did you do about it?*

It never fails. Someone in the audience has faced the same issue, and they would like very much to explain to others how they overcame it. If, by some chance, you are confronted with a question that no one else has the answer, you could respond by saying, *Hmmm, you deserve the best possible answer on that one, and we are a bit stumped right now. I will need to get back with you on that one.*

Be sure to get back with them. Not to worry. That will be a rare case; though it may happen.

If you are going to speak to a group, you want to present yourself as an expert on your topic. Fall in love with you topic. Do not be concerned about being an expert speaker as much as an expert on your topic. Oscar de la Renta, when asked what was his criteria for selecting guests for his parties, he replied, *Passion*. Have a passion for your topic.

The audience should just look at you and think the infor-mation presented to them is merely coming from within you. You want to show them nothing less. So, do not use notes. You are probably thinking, *That's easy for him to say*.

Well, to prove you are right, I will say it again. *Do not use notes.*

Now, let's make it easy for you to do. One mistake speak-ers make is presenting a topic they are not familiar with . . . or perhaps even worse, a topic of which they are not con-vinced. In 1993 while working at a university, I was given the task of selling to university faculty the concept of compressed video. Now, we need to get some things straight. I had never, until the moment I was given the task, heard the term *compressed video.* I had taught at the college level and very much believed in as much experiential learning as possible. A few other staff members and I were to do our selling to faculty . . . that week.

What I read about compressed video at the time was not very convincing. Those views have since changed, but my current view of compressed video did not help me in 1993. While I was attempting to persuade the faculty to buy into the concept of compressed video, the looks on the audience's faces conveyed my tactics were not Academy Award winning caliber.

However, that was not the worst thing that could happen. No one died during my presentation, and I came away with a new idea of a topic that could be presented at symposia no matter the group.

There should be a session at conferences on *Things That Did Not Work.* Everyone has experienced this. Something you tried in your career, but it did not work as planned. In all probability the room would be standing room only. What would be the reason for such a topic? There is probably someone in the room, who tried the same thing but implemented it a little differently and with success.

Baseball Hall of Famer, Ty Cobb, was one of the fiercest competitors in the history of the game. For decades he held the career stolen base record. He once said that he never got caught stealing a base that he did not learn something.

Another Hall of Famer is Hank Aaron. For approximately 30 years Aaron was the all-time career home run leader. Though he hit 755 home runs, which is not too shabby; he also struck out 1,383 times.

Aaron had a routine of after striking out, going back to the dugout and sit-down while pulling his cap over his face. He would look at the pitcher through the one of the air holes in the top of his cap. By doing so, his total focus was on the pitcher. Everything else was blocked out by the cap. He could observe every detail of the pitcher, often finding one flaw in the pitcher's delivery. As an end result, the next time Aaron went to bat, he owned the pitcher.

Perhaps we could employ Aaron's philosophy in many areas of our lives. Learn what did not work, and avoid doing it in the future. That could be with business, relationships, sports, as well as many others.

When speaking to a group, it is a good idea to make them part of your presentation. Ooh, if you are just beginning to speak to groups of people, that idea can be a tall order. No, not really.

When you step onto the stage or from behind the podium . . . I do not like podiums but will discuss that later . . . you look out at faces looking back at you and you see they are expecting something. Sure, they are expecting the information you have prepared, but more importantly, they expect you to be interesting. They want to be entertained. They want to leave your session feeling better about their jobs or themselves. You also want them to leave the session feeling better about you. You might be saying that your audience does not even know you.

That is probably true; consequently, they will start with a neutral feeling about you. It is your job to change that into a positive feeling. You want them to feel a part of your session. How? Just move.

You do not have to know some funny game or activity. Move -- walk around the room. If you walk around the room, people have to turn to see you. If they turn, they will be alert. Besides, very few people go to sleep when they are moving from side to side.

If you want to improve your speaking skills, one of the best ways is to listen -- and watch -- good speakers. Colin Powell said, *It's not your accomplishments that make you successful, it's the people you hang around.*

You will never get better at public speaking by listening to people, who speak worse than you, unless you like telling yourself, *Gee, I sure am glad I'm not that bad.* Even if you are an excellent speaker, you can always learn something from other good speakers that will help to hone your skills.

Tiger Woods is arguably the best golfer on the planet. Whenever he gets in a slump, which granted is not a common experience, what does he do? He visits his golf pro. Is that golf pro a better golfer than Tiger Woods? Not likely. However, he can point out to Woods one aspect of his game that needs work. Woods will practice it over and over until it becomes routine.

Earlier, it was stated to get the audience involved in your program as much as possible. I hear you thinking, *That is easier said than done. I work for a company that sells welders' torches. When I have to speak, there is no way to make my topic exciting!*

That might be true, but I said nothing about making your topic interesting. You need to make your presentation interesting. You might even try this. If you feel your audience is slipping into La La Land, tell them to stand and find someone they do not know.

Give them a minute to do it. Tell them to face their partner and shake their partner's hand. Here's where you say, *Hold on to your partner's hand, look them in the eye and repeat after me, 'If this speaker (pause as the audience repeats your words), gets anymore boring (pause as the audience repeats your words). I am going to slap you naked!'*

Everyone will laugh. It does not matter where you are or who your audience is, after they laugh, your audience will like you. You just make them feel good. When your audience laughs, they purge their stress!

One thing I practice every time I prepare to speak before a group is positive self-talk. Does that work 100% of the time? Absolutely not.

However, negative self-talk does work 100% of the time. I should know. At one time that is the only type of self-talk I ever used with regard to speaking to a group. There was a time when my only concern was getting it over and done as fast as possible. By doing so, my speech was usually even faster, which made it even more difficult to understand. That was many years ago, and long before learning many of the tools speakers use to keep peoples' attention.

Earlier, you read that I do not like podiums. A podium presents a layer between you and your audience. They also convey to the audience that someone is going to stand behind it and from that perch, attempt to fill their need for information.

That is often the type of information that the audience could have read at home. Oh, that reminds me. Never read to an audience. That is an insult. They can read at home. If you can, tell a story. Have the lesson you want to leave with them in the story. Not everyone is a good story teller. So, tell a personal story your audience can relate to. You may say that you do not know such a story. Horse feathers! Tell a story – your story – from your heart. Perhaps your audience would like to relate to you!

You have overcome something in life. Everyone has. Either they have overcome an adversity or they want to know how.

In 1998 I had the privilege of attending a Peter Lowe Seminar. It was six-hours of excellent speakers from Zig Ziglar to Tom Hopkins to Archie Manning.

Lowe shared the story of a young man who knew the importance public speaking has to success in life. However, he possessed none of the traits you normally find in a polished public speaker – deep voice, strong stage presence, the ability to have an audience cling to every word.

Rather, he stuttered and spoke with a lisp. He was never a very good student, failing high school courses and never going to college. His first attempts at public speaking only resulted in humiliation. During one of those first public speeches, he was so nervous that he fainted! He lacked any natural ability to speak in public.

Yet, he was determined to succeed. As mentioned earlier, keep your enemies closer. The fear of public speaking was his enemy. So, he diligently studied the dos and don'ts of public speaking. His studies proved successful. His speeches would ultimately unite a country to fight and with the aid of Allied forces defeat the seemingly indestructible Nazi army. Who was the great speaker? Winston Churchill.

EFFECTIVE COMMUNICATION

WHENEVER I PRESENT a seminar, regardless the program, the subject we are about to discuss is always mentioned. I always tell my audience that it is impossible to retain everything discussed in a seminar. Likewise, I will tell you that it is impossible to retain everything you read in this book.

As my audiences are told, I will tell you that it is imperative for you to retain the information in the upcoming sentences. If you do not retain anything else in this book, you retain the following statement. The key to effective communication -- and the hardest part is -- listening.

Now, am I saying that listening is more important than speaking as a component of communication? Read my lips. . . *Yes*. Listening is an art.

It should not be confused with hearing. If you listen to someone, you give them worth.

The average person listens to 25% of what they hear. It is amazing to think of the excellent presenters that could have given great presentations if they had done the one thing that is the downfall to many a presenter – they opened their mouths. It is difficult for presenters new to the world of public speaking to realize that 55% of a message is body language, 35% is voice and only 7% is words.

Now, read my lips . . . or words . . . the key to effective speaking is . . . *hesitation*. Amazing is it not? The main point

RISE ABOVE

of public speaking involves the mouth being shut. Ah, the
sweet sound of silence.

Listen to speakers, news anchors, evangelists who keep
your attention. They do it with silence . . . by pausing. Tom
Brokaw, Bernard Shaw, Billy Graham, Paul Harvey realized the
key to effective speaking is hesitation. Ever notice what a ner-
vous presenter will do when giving a presentation? He often
speaks like a blue streak. In doing so the words of Voltaire are
realized, *The secret of being a bore is to tell everything*.

His or her message grows faster with words almost piggy-
backing each other. Dionysus said, *Let thy speech be better than
silence, or be silent.*

Too often a presenter will hear someone with notoriety
speak and try to imitate them. Successful speakers do not try to
sound like anyone other than themselves. Being from Missis-
sippi, I have a Southern accent. Dottie Walters of *Sharing Ideas
Newsmagazine* is from the West Coast. She is an expert in the
field of public speaking.

Dottie gave a piece of advice to me during a telephone con-
versation we had that I have adhered ever since -- not to ever
lose my accent. When I am speaking in a northern or western
state, it is common for someone to comment on how much they
just love my accent. Y'all.

An audience thinks visually – and it will help you, the pre-
senter, to think in terms of pictures. Most speeches have very
little impact, because they do not ask you to do anything. A
presentation is a commitment by the presenter to help the audi-
ence do something.

It will help if you picture yourself the captain of the plane
or perhaps a traffic cop. People come to you for help, direction.
Listen to them, to their needs and listen with all of your being.
Give them worth.

Since the late 1960's I have enjoyed the music of B.J.
Thomas. If you need your memory jogged, he is a five-time
Grammy winner, including song of the year in 1969 for *Rain-
drops Keeping Falling on My Head*, which was written by Burt
Bacharach and Hal David.

In November 1993 he was scheduled to perform at the Jones County State Fair in Laurel, MS. This was only a few miles from our home. So on that cool afternoon, my wife Pam and I made the journey to the fairgrounds. We wanted to see and hear this then 51 year-old crooner to see if he still has the talent that garnered those Grammy awards.

His concert was to be under a tent. I found one of the large poles holding up the tent to be vacant – no one else was leaning on it. It was in front of the band. That would be my spot for the concert. B.J. came out singing the song, *No Love at All*. He was incredible.

His band was incredible. He sang all of his hits with several gospel songs sprinkled among his rock & roll hits. How did his voice sound? If anything it had improved. He can still sing at five octaves. Not too shabby. Pam would later tell me that she enjoyed watching me watch him perform.

When the concert was over I told myself that I have got to meet the man. After the concert ended, B.J. went into his bus to freshen-up. He was going to come out and sign autographs at a table near the stage where he just performed.

A rope had been tied to the front of the bus. The rope was stretched along about 20 yards and made a trail for B.J. to walk to the table for autographs and back-of-the-room sales. Ultimately, it was designed to prevent people from getting to B.J. or going near his bus.

In a few minutes B.J. changed clothes and came out of the bus carrying in his hand four black Sharpies used to sign autographs. Standing directly behind the rope about twelve feet from the front of the bus and with hundreds standing behind me, I was perched to say, *Hi* to B.J. as he walked-by.

Four of his crew members walked with him – one to his front, one to his back and one on each side of him. As he got within about four feet of me, I said, *B.J.*

Upon saying this, my expectations were for him to smile, wave at me and continue walking. He did none of the above. He did not smile, nor wave, nor continue walking. He merely stopped in front of me and stared into my face. His four crew members followed suit. Five men were standing still. Each looked at my face.

There was a pause. In that splitz-second I realized – I was in control. They were virtually waiting for me to *make the next move*. My hand went out to him as I said, *You're the best.*

He smiled shook my hand, and said, *Thank you!*

We continued to shake hands. I again said, *The best!*

He smiled even more and said another convincing, *Thank you!*

I had to stop the handshake. He paused, smiled and continued his walk to the autograph table.

Please realize what just happened. I paid money to hear him sing, but the high point was when he listened to me. When B.J. listened to me, he was conveying to me that I had worth.

If all he did was hear me, the scenario mentioned earlier – smile, wave, continue walking, would have occurred. Rather, he listened to me with his entire being. Did he gain anything by doing that? That day and because of what had happened I joined his fan club. He made money from listening to me.

Later, I met B.J.'s lead guitar player, Daryl Hoffman. We spoke as he was putting his guitar in its case. He presented himself as a very friendly down to earth fellow. After we visited for a few moments, Pam and I walked away from Daryl. As I turned around, I noticed that he was following us.

Whenever we walked by another band member, Daryl would motion to the band member and say, *Hey, this is Greg and Pam Little.*

We met all the band members that day, because one band member found worth in us.

As stated earlier, when you listen to someone, you are giving to them – worth. Who do you think of most often? If asked that question aloud during a workshop, you may reply, *My kids, grandkids, spouse, girlfriend, boyfriend or perhaps God.*

Nope. You think about you more than anyone else. You better. No one is going to lookout for you as much as you are.

When you convey to someone that you want to know about them, you are letting them know that they have worth to you.

You will soon read about my good friend, Dr. Dale Henry. Dale and I did our doctoral study together in the late 80's and early 90's.

He is now a speaker, and has provided seminars and workshops in all of the United States, cruise ships and other countries. The way Dale progressed in the public speaking profession is mind-boggling. He no longer advertises. There is no need.

All of his promotion is now word of mouth. There is one exception, when he will book a workshop not by word of mouth. He will fly to or from one of his programs and will be sitting with someone one a plane. They might get into the usual small talk. Then Dale will start enquiring about his fellow passenger, i.e., is he married, have kids or what does he do for a living.

As his fellow passenger tells of his or her exploits in business and family, Dale will listen – intently. He will smile, nod, and ask questions about the other person's topic. Then, as the plane lands, Dale is asked what he does. Dale gives his big Tennessee grin and says, *Oh, I'm a speaker.*

As he pulls out one of his videos he hands it to his new friend and says, *Here, take this and when you have a little time, take a look at it.*

The passenger smiles and takes Dale's tape. As Dale is walking through the airport, he phones his secretary, Michelle, and tells her to expect a call from (the contact's name) to book a program. He has this thing, *listening*, down to an art form.

The past few pages we have talked about public speaking or at least parts of public speaking. How is that related to with overcoming adversity? Much has been said about the art of listening and giving worth to people. A very good way to overcome an adversity is to do something that will enhance the quality of someone else's life.

What you actually will be doing is enhancing the quality of your life. When you do this, you are defocusing on any adversity you have and focusing on another's needs. When you become a worth builder or value finder of people, an adversity you may have is diminished.

When developing my first six-hour workshop in 1985, the first thing I had to decide is what I wanted to accomplish with my presentation. I had to find the right audience for the activities I wanted to present. It was to be a full-day workshop for professionals working in long-term health care facilities in Mississippi.

At the time there were approximately 220 long-term care facilities in the state. Letters were sent to all long-term health care settings. The audience would be primarily activity directors and social workers from all over the state. What did I want to accomplish? I wanted the attendees to *see* and participate in — not just hear — realistic age-appropriate activities they could provide their residents.

Months were spent developing the workshop. I went over well more than 110 activities until I could do them in my sleep . . . and I may have! The material was reviewed until each one could be discussed and implemented with confidence. Note that I said, *discussed*, not memorized. In doing this, some items were omitted and many refined. Constantly prune your weeds and things that no longer belong in your programs.

If you are going to speak to a group, decide what you want to achieve with your presentation. Years ago, I heard a man speak at an employee of the year ceremony. He gave a story about a basketball coach, who had his team really pumped up going into a big game. They stormed out of the locker room sensing sure victory. After they were on the basketball court, all of the players stopped in disbelief. There were no goals up. The backboards stood at each end of the court empty of the little round things with the nets hanging down. The players asked, *What are we suppose to do?*

They asked, *How will we know if we win? How will anyone know if we are winning? How can we measure our success?*

Without goals we do not know where we are going. Always set your goals, as well as the objectives to reach those goals. Make sure your goals and objectives are measurable. You are the change agent. Your job is to change your audiences' actions and/or attitudes. When that has been accomplished, learning has occurred.

Still afraid that public speaking is not your *cup of tea?* You might be right. Remember, there was one time in my life that it was suggested that I work with individuals with hearing impairments, because by doing so, I would not have to talk very much.

What if I had adhered to that suggestion? I would not have presented seminars in the majority of the United States, and you would not be holding this book. There was also a time, when I really considered working with the individuals with hearing impairments.

My speech impediment was that dominant in my life. Now I have come to see the truth in the words of Mark Twain. Specifically, *Keep away from people who try to belittle your ambitions. Small people always do that, but really great people make you feel that you, too, can become great.*

One might think that it was discouraging for me to hear during my first visit with my speech therapist that I could not be *cured.* On the contrary after learning the rules to overcome this adversity, it gave control to me. I was in control of my speech . . . whether I use the controls or not.

Having a speech impediment for decades, I had convinced myself that getting it *fixed* would be an enormous undertaking. Then during my first day of therapy I was informed that it could not be *fixed.* Rather, I would be given the tools to control my speech, and only I can use the controls. Having to use the tools whenever I open my mouth would be an awesome task.

Perhaps you would like to know what the hardest part of all was. It was realizing and accepting the fact that it was really easy to do, if I use the tools. I just had to accept that I was in the driver's seat.

ALONG CAME DALE

THE SUMMER OF 1989 began my journey toward a terminal degree in Adult and Continuing Education. Reviewing all of the requirements for a doctoral degree was an overwhelming experience.

Coursework, which would include statistics and a foreign language; a comprehensive examination and a dissertation, all would come while working full-time at a facility treating individuals with chemical dependency and at times individuals with mental illness. It should be pointed out that I was not the Lone Ranger. Most of my fellow doctoral students also worked full-time while going to school.

During that initial semester I was befriended by another doctoral student. He was from Tennessee. Dale Henry. If you have not met Dale, he can be difficult to describe.

That first semester he lived in a small trailer, actually the word *small* does not do it justice, with another doctoral student, Isidor Muniz from South Carolina but with a Puerto Rican descent. How these two *train wrecks* ever met, I'm sure I don't know. Perhaps it's best for you to know that Dale went home each weekend to his wife and two girls.

Anyway, Dale and I developed a friendship from the beginning. He was in the Air Force Reserves. The only time he did not wear cowboy boots to class was when he had a reserve meeting. Dale is a bit vertically challenged, but he was born with a smile frozen to his face, which made up for the lack of height. He's not really short – just not very tall.

We studied through our coursework, prepared for tests, and somehow were able to get through statistics and French together. Whenever I would get stressed and think the only light I see at the end of the tunnel is a head-on train, Dale would pat me on the back and assuredly say with a huge smile, *Greg, it's going to be ok.*

He was always positive. It is somehow comforting to hear from someone facing the same challenges you're facing that things are going to be ok. Dale taught vocational training at a small institution, but the oldest college in Tennessee. As it turned out, things were going to be ok for Dale as well.

Dale finished his Ph.D. in 1991. Due to Drew's illness and ultimate death, my Ph.D. was not completed until December 1992. Marching directly after me in the commencement exercise was my friend, Isidor *Izzy* Muniz. Izzy and I kept in touch and still see each other once a year. However, for a few years I heard nothing from Dale. I had wondered what had happened to the small fellow with the over-sized grin.

Then one night my phone rang. It's was Dale, but he seemed different. His speech had lost its Southern drawl. He asked how I was doing then asked me if I knew what he was doing. Well, I thought he was now the dean of his college. He said, *No. I quit.*

Now I'm thinking, *Oh no. He's called for a loan!* (Not really, but it sounds funny.)

He then said something I would have never imagined coming from his mouth. He had gone into full-time public speaking. The college where he was working had Dale flying to different cities giving speeches. One night on a flight home, Dale said to himself, *Why do I have to do this for them? I can do this for myself.*

I asked, *When you quit your job at the college, how many speaking engagements did you have booked?*

He replied, *None.*

Hearing that, I knew I was speaking to the right Dale Henry! Only the Dale I know would have done that. Dale believed in himself. People can believe in you. Your spouse, parent, children or co-workers, but if you don't believe in yourself, you will stay right where you are.

Dale went on to tell me that he had presented seminars in 46 states and wanted to send one of his VCR tapes to me. That was in the late '90's. He has now spoken in all 50 states, other countries, cruise ships, has shared the stage with many celebrities and become friends with people like Zig Ziglar, Lou Holtz, Dolly Parton and others. Whenever I get discouraged, I phone Dale, because I know by the end of our conversation, he's going to say, *Greg, it's going to be alright.*

I advise you to do that. Surround yourself with people who affirm you. Avoid negative people . . . they are going nowhere. If you want to improve in anything, such as, golf, public speaking, anything, do those things with people who do it better than you. You will never learn how to improve a skill from someone who functions at a skill level below you.

Every year or two, I try to visit Dale and his family. They live in a house in Tennessee overlooking the Smoky Mountains. He always has that smile glued to his face and has the uncanny ability to make people laugh, which means that he makes other people smile . . . with a little volume.

I have had opportunity to hear and see Dale train professionals on many occasions. Though he keeps his audiences glued to his every word, his strongest ability is relating to people . . . regardless of their position in life.

THE POWER YOU HAVE

YOU MAY HAVE heard the saying, *Be kind to everyone, because everyone is fighting some sort of a battle*. Everyone wants to feel better. Some may brag about what they've done or what they have. That's often to camouflage the fact there is something missing in their life.

As stated earlier, that missing element leaves a gap. It could be from low self-esteem, disappointments, a broken relationship, failure at work or school, . . . everyone has gaps. Everyday try to fill someone's emotional gap. There is no need to look for someone with a need. Just be open and willing. It will happen.

Right now, look at your thumb. You heard me . . . well, read me . . . look at your thumb. There is literally no thumb like your thumb in the entire universe. Sir Isaac Newton stated there is enough awesomeness in the thumb to prove there is a God. What your thumb has done in your lifetime is mind boggling. Whether you knew it or not your thumb has touched someone in a way that changed their life in a positive manner forever. That someone will never forget you for doing that. You probably don't even know it.

You might be thinking, *Well, I do know someone I helped in a powerful way*. That may be true, but there is something else you did for someone else that you do not even know you did it. . . but they do.

In the spring on 2007 a lovely lady came into my life. Her husband had died of cancer not too many months before we met. We began spending a great deal of time together and fell in love. Soon afterwards, we got engaged but had planned the *getting married* part slowly.

She had three grown kids and seven grandchildren. She also had four dogs, Shih Tzus, which I adored . . . and they adored me. After being engaged for the greater part of a year, we realized that just because two people are in love does not mean they should necessarily plan a lifetime together. We separated on very good terms, and I continue to have a great deal of respect for her.

One afternoon while we were engaged, she and I went out for dinner with her younger daughter, Holly. As I talked about the book I was writing, I shared with Holly some of these adversities mentioned in the book.

Holly learned of me going through my academic years with a severe speech impediment and how I was able to survive a motor vehicle accident, which resulted in an 8-day coma and having to relearn how to walk and talk. Then she learned of my infant son dying after a lengthy illness. After hearing all this, Holly said, *Wow, Greg! What you've done is incredible. Just imagine how much more you could have done had you not had all those challenges.*

And my thought, *What I accomplished. . . would have been less.*

REFERENCES

Ader, R., Felton, D., & Nicholas, R. (1981).
Psychoneuromuniology. New York: Academic Press, Inc.

Cousins, N. (1979). Anatomy of an illness. New York: W.W.
Norton & Company, Inc.

Griessman, G. (1993). The Achievement factors. San Diego:
Pfeiffer & Company.

Metcalf, C.W. (1988) Humor, risk & change. (Audiotape).
Fort Collins, CO: C.W. Metcalf and Company.

Morgan, R. (1972, June 19). Trapped youth remains poor.
Daily Corinthian. p. 5.

Morris, M.G. (2004, May 14). Hundreds learn more about
mental health. Tupelo Daily Journal. P. 4A.

Parker, R.S. (1990). Traumatic brain injury and neuropsycho-
logical impairment. New York: SpringerVerlag.

Phend, C. (2010, October 4). Genetic origins of stuttering
uncovered with surprising results. MedPage Today.